Staying in the Game

Providing Social Opportunities for Children and Adolescents with Autism Spectrum Disorders and Other Developmental Disabilities

By

James W. Loomis, Ph.D.

Autism Asperger Publishing Company
P.O. Box 23173
Shawnee Mission, Kansas 66283-0173
www.asperger.net

©2008 Autism Asperger Publishing Company
P. O. Box 23173
Shawnee Mission, Kansas 66283-0173
www.asperger.net • 877-288-8254

Publisher's Cataloging-in-Publication

Loomis, James W.
    Staying in the game : providing social opportunities for children and adolescents with autism spectrum disorders and other developmental disabilities / by James W. Loomis. -- Shawnee Mission, Kan. : Autism Asperger Pub. Co., c2008.

        p. ; cm.
        ISBN: 978-1-934575-29-1
        LCCN: 2008930913
        Includes bibliographical references and index.

        1. Autistic children--Behavior modification. 2. Autistic youth--Behavior modification. 3. Social skills in children--Study and teaching. 4. Social interaction in children--Study and teaching. 5. Social participation--Study and teaching. 6. Autism in children. 7. Autism in adolescence. I. Title. II. Social opportunities for children and adolescents with autism spectrum disorders.

RJ506.A9 L66 2008   2008930913
618.92/85882--dc22   0808

Cover art: ©istockphoto; Tom Nulens

Printed in the United States of America

Acknowledgments

This book would not have been possible without input from the many individuals with whom I have worked, along with their families and the school teams that served them. These people have generously shared their experience and wisdom and have taught me so much about disability, social development, life in schools, and autism.

I also want to acknowledge Lisa Mann's excellent editorial support. Her valuable contributions helped put the manuscript into a more useful format and made it easier to understand.

Over the years I have benefited from my own set of "peer mentors," who have provided encouragement and shared their expertise, including Michael Powers, Linda Hudson, and Lois Rosenwald. I am very grateful for their support.

Finally, I want to express my appreciation for the support of my family: my wife, Carol, and my daughters, Rebecca and Kathryn.

– James W. Loomis

Table of Contents

Introduction

Families and schools today are confronted with growing numbers of children and adolescents with autism spectrum disorders and other developmental disabilities. For reasons that are not yet well understood, the frequency of autistic disorders appears to be increasing. Further, improvement in diagnostic techniques is allowing many high-functioning students to be appropriately identified and treated. With improved early intervention services, there is also a growing group of children with more serious disabilities who have developed the skills to function adaptively in less restricted settings.

Despite gains in many areas for almost all of these students, social functioning is a key area of challenge. Many are socially isolated from peers and have difficulty with managing day-to-day interactions with teachers and other staff. Struggles with communication skills, perspective-taking, social problem-solving, and mastering the "hidden curriculum" make it difficult for them to enjoy relationships and take advantage of learning opportunities within a social format. For many of these students, it is the development of social competencies, even more than academic or vocational skills, that will determine how independent they can be as adults.

A lot is written about social skills training for these students, including many innovative and creative approaches to teaching key skills. However, the research literature cautions us that while it is feasible to successfully teach many social skills to students, it is very difficult to have them apply what they learn outside of the teaching context or group. Children will be able to demonstrate the skills in the group, class, or session, but that does not translate to using them on the playground, in the cafeteria, or in the neighborhood where it really counts. And, if they do not use these skills outside of the teaching context, they are eventually forgotten and lost.

This challenge is known as *generalization* – applying learned skills in different settings and situations when needed. Generalization has been difficult to establish for social skills interventions with a wide range of children, but it is particularly tough for children with autism spectrum disorders (e.g., Gresham, 2002; Schreibman & Ingersoll, 2005). Their learning can be very context-based such that they only demonstrate behaviors or skills with the person who taught them or in the setting where they were learned.

This book addresses this challenge by presenting a range of interventions aimed at promoting generalization of social skills. It is intended to complement the many curricula, programs, and interventions that have been developed to teach social skills to children with autism spectrum disorders and other developmental disabilities (e.g., Baker, 2003; Bellini, 2006; Coucouvanis, 2004; McAfee, 2002; Winner, 2002). In many schools, children participate in a social skills group or "lunch bunch" but little else. Consequently, while they are learning social competencies, they have no opportunities to practice or generalize the skills. This book presents ways to establish social situations that can be opportunities for generalization.

The book focuses on children from kindergarten through high school who are programmed within the mainstream on a part- or full-time basis. Many of the strategies can also be applied in self-contained special education classrooms. However, they are directed at settings where the goal is to promote integration and inclusion of the child in social activities with typical children. The students discussed in this book demonstrate basic social recognition, communication skills, a tolerance of peers, and even some interest or desire to interact with them. And their behavior is under sufficient control for them to effectively participate in learning and social activities.

The interventions can be useful with a range of children with developmental disabilities. This includes autism spectrum disorders (i.e., autism, Asperger Syndrome, high-functioning autism, pervasive developmental disorders-not otherwise specified [PDD-NOS], nonverbal learning disabilities, semantic and pragmatic disorders, and some children with intellectual disabilities). It is designed for students who can master social competencies in a teaching context but need support to apply the skills throughout their day.

Written for school personnel and parents, the book includes interventions for both school and home/community. The emphasis is on the school environment because this is perhaps the most important forum for the development of social skills and because the presence of trained staff and other resources allows for many interventions that would not be possible in the community.

The model presented in this book is consistent with the theory and practices of inclusion and integrating students with special needs into the mainstream. The focus is on going beyond just placing students in the mainstream, to taking advantage of inclusion by facilitating the use of typical students to address the generalization of social skills, one of the most profound challenges of autism and other developmental disabilities

Even when the interventions presented here have been found to be effective in educational and clinical work, it is important to note that there has not been much empirical research examining the efficacy of these programs. One goal of this book is to spur further applications as well as investigations into their benefits.

How to Use This Book

In Chapter 1, we begin by presenting the principles upon which this work is based and describing a model to guide our efforts. Chapters 2 and 3 look at the process of identifying and assessing social opportunities and ensuring success in them. The following four chapters each addresses one type of intervention: group-based work (Chapter 4), interventions by staff and parents (Chapter 5), using peer mentors (Chapter 6), and adapting extracurricular activities (Chapter 7). Chapter 8 concludes with an overview of the process of providing social opportunities.

Note

To facilitate the ease of reading, several protocols have been followed. Students are referred to using masculine pronouns and teachers using feminine pronouns. The term *typical* is used to refer to the body of students who do not present autism spectrum or related disorders. At times the terms *child* and *children* are used generically to include adolescents. Finally, while the approach presented in this book is applicable to a wide range of individuals with developmental disabilities (including nonverbal learning disabilities), the text typically refers to just individuals with autism spectrum disorders. This choice of usage is in no way intended to de-emphasize the importance of respecting and supporting all individuals, regardless of gender, disability/diagnosis, or age.

Preface

It was a high-stakes game of Four Square on the playground at recess. A mix of fourth and fifth graders was playing – a couple of girls, but predominantly boys. Most of the kids were just going through the motions. They would have their turn in the D square, but they were no match for the four or five star players who dominated the game every day.

The trickiest, most cunning player was Joey. He was one of the smallest kids in the game, but he spent a lot of time in the A square because he had the best mix of shots – "slammies," "high bouncers," and "double slaps." He'd devised most of the shots himself and given them names so the other kids would admire them and want to try them. Joey was also the master of fast starts (before people were ready), distractions, and mid-match rule changes that gave him even more of an advantage.

The strongest kid was Brian. He was a good six inches taller than everyone else in the game, broad shouldered, with strong arms and legs. He always wore a knit hat and a black t-shirt. Brian didn't like to talk a lot. But then, he didn't have to. One glaring look from him, and the other kids would go along with whatever he wanted. Even Joey didn't dare to argue with Brian.

Seth was a student with an autism spectrum disorder. He could talk and do most of the schoolwork that the other kids did, and he spent most of his day in the general education classroom with help from an aide. Seth didn't really spend much time thinking about the other kids. He preferred to play with certain toys and to do things that he could control and repeat over and over and over. However, over the past couple of years he had begun to notice the games that the other children were playing and become interested in joining.

Since starting fourth grade this year, Seth had been playing Four Square regularly. He waited in line until his turn, stepped up to the D square, and was quickly dispatched by a hard shot, a high-bouncing shot, or a low quick shot. At first, that didn't bother him. He liked the repetition and the routine – wait in line, step up, miss the shot, wait in line, step up, miss the shot, and so on. But lately, he had been watching the other children in the A, B, and C squares and seen how, when one kid missed, everyone else got to move up the ladder. Now, Seth wanted to move into the higher squares, too. He was beginning to see that not getting beyond the D square was "failure." He wanted to succeed.

On this particular day, the game started as usual. The usual kids dominated and took turns in the A and B squares. Joey was being particularly tricky and was hanging on to the A square for an extended period of time. Brian was in the B square and holding his own. Seth took his turn waiting in line, each time quickly getting eliminated. He already had been having a bad day. He hated the division problems they were doing in math. And the aide had yelled at him when she caught him playing with his pencil box and he couldn't find his homework. His frustration was growing, and the Four Square game was making it worse.

The first time he was eliminated, he stamped his foot and said "Oh, man!" The second time, he hopped up and down several times and flapped his arms as he walked back to the line. Each time he was eliminated, his behavior got worse, and he lost a little more control. The other kids noticed, but they had seen it before. A girl whispered, "It's alright, Seth." But you could tell that this was going to escalate into a problem. Seth was going to lose it, and there was going to be trouble. Several of the kids looked around for a teacher, but all the adults were at the other end of the playground.

Seth got ready to take his turn again. He was doing a little hand flap but trying to focus on the game. Before he even settled in, that trickster Joey pulled one of his meanest and best moves – a quick start. He quickly threw the ball across the corner of Seth's square before Seth even knew what was happening. He sealed the deal by yelling "Ha! You're out! You're out! You're out!" Seth stood flapping his arms, staring into space. All the kids watched. They knew that he was going to lose it big time.

But it didn't happen. Instead, the kids' attention was shifted from Seth to the B square. Brian, the strong, quiet kid, softly said, "Seth wasn't ready. It's a do-over." The crowd was dumbfounded. Joey stared at Brian. He was furious that Brian was undermining one of his best tricks. He knew better than to take on Brian, but he wasn't done yet. When the ball was retrieved and returned to Joey, he did another quick start to Seth, again pronouncing "You're out! You're out! You're out!"

Seth stood dumbfounded for a moment, then looked at Brian. All the other kids looked at Brian, too. After a couple of seconds, Brian, uncomfortable with all the attention, quietly said to Joey, "Illegal serve. You crossed the line. You're out." That was more than Joey could stand. He began to talk fast, citing rules (real and made up), and insisting that he was still in A square and that Seth was out. Brian slowly began to walk to the A square. The kids watched and then, in a choir of retorts, declared that, indeed, Joey was out.

With Joey out of the A square, Brian served to the B and C square players, and Seth actually survived several rounds and made it briefly to the B square. When he was finally eliminated, he smiled as he calmly walked to the end of the line, very much enjoying the feeling of success.

Scenes like this occur every day at elementary schools across the country. For children, playing games, developing roles, and negotiating/arguing are essential parts of social development. Through this and many other types of social activity, children learn how to talk to peers, play with peers, make friends, resolve conflicts, and have fun.

In this particular situation, Seth was practicing a number of social skills that he had worked hard to learn over the preceding years, including turn-taking, respecting personal space in crowds, making small talk, and managing frustration. Some of these skills were learned in his social skills group, some from his parents, and some he'd figured out on his own. One truly exciting aspect of this incident was that Seth had a chance to apply and practice these skills within his peer group – and that the peer group was supporting his efforts (as they are with most typical children). There were no teachers or staff members telling the children what to do; yet, instead of teasing and rejection, there was inclusion and support.

A key challenge for children with autism spectrum disorders and other developmental disabilities is that they are excluded from these social opportunities for many different reasons. They may not have the communication or social skills to keep up and participate. They may be victimized by teasing or bullying. Well-meaning adults may isolate them in order to protect them from rejection. In fact, a year before this event took place, Seth spent all his time at recess alone, walking around the perimeter of the playground, talking to himself and looking for pebbles.

Seth had worked hard at his social skills training, both at home and at school. But lessons weren't enough. It took a schedule of structured, supported social opportunities, designed and implemented by Seth's school team and parents, before Seth was able to start interacting with his peer group. It was those same opportunities that allowed Seth's peers to become comfortable with him, despite his obvious differences, and start including him in their games and interactions ... their shared process of social skill development. These efforts to create social opportunities are what this book is about.

Chapter 1

A Model for Providing Social Opportunities

- *The importance of generalization*
- *Creating social opportunities*
- *Practical considerations*

ocial skills training can be an effective way of teaching new skills to children with autism spectrum disorders (ASDs). Research has established that. The problem is, these children typically don't *generalize* their new skills – meaning they don't turn around and use them in the real world, where it counts (e.g., Gresham, 2002; Timler, Vogler-Elias, & McGill, 2007). That's not surprising, when you think about it. Would you teach a child to swim in a shallow, calm pool and then just drop him into a stormy ocean and expect him to stay afloat? Of course not. But far too often, adults expect children with ASDs to walk out of social skills training and be able to apply a newly learned skill on a busy playground or in a noisy cafeteria.

Children need a progression from *easy* to *gradually more difficult* settings in order to test out new skills, become comfortable with them, and then apply them with greater ease and competence. They need a level of *built-in supports that are gradually reduced* until no longer needed.

This type of approach is built into most academic teaching in schools. Take math, for instance. You start out teaching addition and give the child a lot of practice in this area before you ask him to move on to subtraction or multiplication. You outline the steps of an operation and slowly walk the student through it, one step at a time, before expecting him to navigate it on his own.

Generalization can be thought of as a path from where the skill is taught to the "natural setting" where it would typically occur. Social skills may be taught in a number of settings, from a 1:1 instructional session in a cubby to a social skills training group. But if a child's actually going to master these new skills, he'll need to gradually begin using them outside his training setting, moving from settings where it is easier to demonstrate the skill to situations where it is more difficult. And to ensure success, he'll need varying levels of support along the way. Ultimately, the goal is for the child to be able to use his new skills where the real social interactions occur – in the hallways at school, on the playground, at a friend's house, and in the community.

Behavioral research into generalization generally focuses on instructional or training techniques, such as making the treatment environment similar to the natural environment or teaching a wide range of stimulus conditions and response requirements. It also emphasizes the importance of reinforcers occurring in the natural environment (e.g., Cooper, Heron, & Heward, 2007). This book addresses the latter – *how to create social environments that are supportive of and reinforcing to the child's exercise of social skills.*

How Adults Drop the Ball

Because children with ASDs and other developmental disabilities need help generalizing social skills, we adults need to make sure that they get to practice them in a variety of social settings. That doesn't sound too complicated, right? But actually, there are a number of ways in which teams and parents seem to go astray, including the following:

- **Letting the child fend for himself.** Many adults think that the child doesn't need help or should be left to his own choices and devices, including being as social or as isolated as he wants. This typically leads to the child either withdrawing from others (e.g., walking around the edges of the playground by himself, looking at bugs), or attempting to socialize, but in an odd or awkward manner that annoys peers and leads to conflict, teasing, and behavior problems. Either way, the child doesn't get a chance to practice and master the social skills that he'll need later in life. Instead, he gets left behind and becomes more and more isolated. (This is frequently the case with children who go undiagnosed, or whose educational teams underestimate the severity of their social challenges.)

- **Providing social activities that are *too challenging*.** Some well-meaning teams work to involve the child in social activities, but then don't provide enough support or structure for the child to be successful. Rejection, scapegoating, and conflict are often the result. Not surprisingly, this leads to frustration, behavior problems, and, ultimately, loss of social motivation.

- **Providing social activities that are *not challenging enough*.** Many adults see the social vulnerability in children with ASDs and become overprotective. As a result, they may set up social activities, but with too much support and not enough challenge. In these situations, the child's social motivation is supported, but he doesn't learn the skills that will allow him to independently participate in social activities with his peers. Moreover, these well-meaning adults may tolerate – and advise the other children to tolerate – inappropriate behaviors (e.g., hugging, interrupting, or silliness) that will hurt the child socially in other situations.

The Objective: Creating Appropriate Social Opportunities

So it's clear that just sticking a child in with a group of peers or well-meaning adults isn't going to be enough to help him generalize and master his social skills. But how *do* you go about putting together a program of activities that will help him meet those goals?

There are several key elements. The child needs to be involved in a *variety of regular social opportunities* where he will *successfully participate*, *practice his social skills*, and *enjoy himself.*

Engaging in a Variety of Regular Social Opportunities

There is no "right" amount of social activity to prescribe. Some people prefer to be social all day long, and others prefer solitary pursuits. But students with ASDs do usually learn best through *repeated exposure* to tasks or challenges. First they need to become familiar with a situation. Then they can practice the steps of what they need to do in that situation … multiple times. Under these conditions, they can master many tough challenges.

With that in mind, to make sure social skills generalize, you need to provide *multiple opportunities* for social practice *every day*.

While you can support the child's need to be by himself for periods of time, you must build in social opportunities where they naturally occur. For example, you would like to see some social practice during lunch, recess, in the hallway between classes, and in the community on the weekend. Depending on the child's level of functioning, these may need to be short, highly structured interactions, or there may be some longer, more complex ones, but they need to happen regularly in order to allow generalization and maintenance of skills.

You also need to address the child's difficulties with applying what he learns in *different settings* and with *different types of people*. That means providing practice opportunities in a range of situations with various people. For example, you might want to include interactions involving playing at recess, greeting people in the community, participating in a play date, being a member of a club or team, talking with teachers and school staff, and so forth.

Some people ask if it's better for the child to practice with typical peers or with other children with special needs. Or whether it's preferable for the child to interact with same-age peers, rather than with adults or younger children. The answer to these questions is that *all social practice is good social practice.* But you want *variety*, so that the child can apply his skills to interactions with a range of people.

Usually, children with ASDs find it easier to practice social skills with adults or younger children. Adults tend to be more tolerant of, and patient with, a child's communication difficulties. Younger children communicate in a simpler, more straightforward manner themselves, which makes it easier. The most difficult interaction – for *all* children – is reciprocal interaction with typical, same-age peers, because it places the greatest demands on verbal and nonverbal communications skills. When peers talk, there is an expectation that they will be able to easily understand each other's messages (verbal and nonverbal). Because of these expectations, peers tend to be the least tolerant of poor social skills. On the other hand, this type of "symmetric" relationship between equals can lead to the greatest intimacy, emotional sharing, and friendship. Furthermore, being skillful with same-age peer relationships is particularly important, because that's the type of relationship that predominates for independent adults – in personal relationships, in the workplace, and so on.

However, same-age interactions with typical peers are not the only type of interaction that people have. Other types of relationships are also important and should be encouraged. In social skill training groups containing only children with special needs, wonderful relationships often develop between group members (see Baker, 2003). A key component of these friendships is the realization that both members experience certain challenges and see the world in a certain way that "typicals just don't get." This type of bond doesn't occur with nondisabled peers.

To best promote generalization, all types of social opportunities should be pursued. If certain types of interaction are missing, then try to find opportunities in those areas. If there is a lot of interaction with just adults, just family members, just girls, or just peers with special needs, don't devalue these opportunities or restrict them. Instead, try to add new experiences that will further diversify the child's experience.

Successful Participation

"Successful participation" means meeting the social demands of a given situation; that is, fitting in, following the important social rules, and interacting in a way that is satisfying to others. Here you are confronting a difficult truth: Social competence is ultimately subjective. That is, how well you perform socially is "in the eye of the beholder." It is the reaction of the people with whom you interact that determines your success or failure. More troubling is the fact that, from a very early age, children prefer to interact with others who are socially competent; that is, peers who leave them socially satisfied (e.g., Stone & LaGreca, 1986).

So in your efforts to promote generalization of social skills, "successful participation" is essential. It doesn't matter whether a child carries out a social interaction by using speech, body language, or an augmentative communication device; what matters is that the interaction leaves the other person feeling good about how it went and looking forward to future interactions. "Successful participation" is essential to being accepted by peers, and the child is going to need those peers. After all, you cannot experience social activities by yourself.

Social development is not a simple, straightforward progression. Social skills in all areas (e.g., greetings, conversation, game play, forming friendships) evolve over the course of development, become more complex and reciprocal, and look different at each age. Ongoing participation in the social environment requires being able to use skills at or close to the level of the peer group. In preschool, age-expected social skills are fairly simple, emphasizing sharing, turn-taking, social bids, and interactive imaginary play. The requirements grow in complexity through elementary school, as the ability to carry on a conversation, interpret facial expressions and body language, negotiate compromises, read social context, and join groups all become more and more essential to success. Expectations then take a big leap in middle school and high school, when a teen needs to know how to form closer, intimate relationships; manage cliques; extend invitations to others (it's totally uncool for Mom to arrange play dates for a 14-year-old!); and follow the unwritten rules of dress, jargon, and social behavior. In other words, social competency is a "moving target," and you have to keep up in order to participate.

Therefore, keeping the child "in the game" and preventing him from falling too far behind becomes a key objective. Most children with ASDs will always struggle with social demands and remain "quirky" and unique. And that's okay. The goal is not to make them the most popular kids in school or to make them act like everybody else. Rather, it's to give them the skills they need to be able to participate with peers in activities that are enjoyable for everyone.

Kids on the spectrum are always at risk of falling into a "vicious cycle" (see Figure 1-1). As they lag behind in their social development, the peer group is more likely to reject them. The more they are rejected, the fewer opportunities they get to practice their social skills. The less they practice, the further behind they fall. And so on and so on ... In order to avoid this vicious cycle and to keep the child in the social game, you must work to create "successful" social experiences.

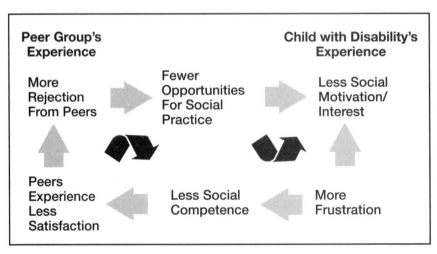

Figure 1-1: Opportunities to Practice Social Skills – A Vicious Cycle

Practicing Social Skills

Another essential element of social opportunities is that they allow the child to practice key social skills. The child needs to exercise each new skill in different settings if he's going to get comfortable with it and master it well enough to use it regularly.

It's not unusual for children with ASDs to *participate* in social situations without actually *practicing* their social skills. For example, during family occasions, a child may participate and interact with a range of relatives. However, they may tolerate his interruptions, abrupt shifts in topic, endless lectures about his special interests, or silly, immature behaviors. In fact, they may even encourage them if they think they're cute or entertaining. By contrast, during recess, the child may tag along with his peer group, but remain on the periphery, watching what is going on, but not actually talking to or playing with the other kids.

Situations like these may help a child become more comfortable around others, or even learn a little about appropriate behavior (although learning through observation does not tend to be a strength for children with ASDs; e.g., Rogers, Cook, & Meryl, 2005). But they may also support bad habits such as interrupting, hogging a conversation, or self-isolation.

You want to find social opportunities that allow the child to practice the social skills that he has learned in group. If the demands are too easy and he can get by without using his social skills, or if they're too difficult and he gets overwhelmed, either way he's not going to get the practice he needs to become more socially competent.

Deriving Enjoyment from Social Interactions

Few children on the autism spectrum feel a lot of motivation to socialize with their peers (e.g., Carter, Davis, Klin, & Volkmar, 2005; Schopler & Mesibov, 1986). Often, they'd rather explore certain objects or sensations, recite scripted monologues, or work at stockpiling facts about their special interests. Many of these kids don't really get lonely or feel a strong urge to play and interact with others, especially when they're younger. Even when they are motivated to interact, they generally view processing social information, communicating with people, and remembering all the unwritten social rules (e.g., maintaining personal space, speaking softly) as a lot of work. And then, when they *do* try to socialize, their awkward social skills may inadvertently alienate or even offend others, so that instead of being rewarded for their efforts, they get rejected or teased.

That's why it's vital that you make the child's social activities enjoyable – *worth the effort*. (In behavioral terms, make them "reinforcing.") For most children with these challenges, you'll find that social experiences become more enjoyable and satisfying as they develop more skills. As they become better able to communicate, carry on back-and-forth conversations, and join in their peers' games and activities, they come to find the joys of social contact and friendship. But for many students, past attempts to socialize have only resulted in frustration, confusion, and rejection. So particularly at first, you, the adult, must work to make sure the social practice opportunities are as enjoyable as possible.

You can't order a child to "go practice your social skills" each night the way you might tell him to go practice the piano, so you'll need to support whatever social motivation he has, however slight. Some kids yearn for friends or dates. Others have more specific goals, such as stopping their classmates from teasing them, having a person to sit with at lunch, or having someone to listen while they talk about their special interests. But many children will not be able to come up with *any* reason why they'd want to interact with peers. That's where you come in.

While you want to nurture whatever social motivations your child has (and to a certain extent, use these motivations to direct your focus), they likely won't be sufficient for our purposes. You'll need to augment those motivations by making social opportunities enjoyable, in and of themselves. You do this by:

- ▶ ensuring that the social demands aren't too high and don't require too much effort,
- ▶ using a lot of humor, games, and fun activities,
- ▶ incorporating the child's special interests,
- ▶ including people he likes, and
- ▶ framing the activity in positive, exciting, or enjoyable terms (rather than as "practice" or "work").

If it seems like a lot of work to create enjoyable social opportunities for a child who would just prefer to be by himself, remember that for many children on the spectrum, social motivation grows in adolescence (e.g., Carter et al., 2005; Schopler & Mesibov, 1986), so "keeping them in the game" is well worth the effort. Many adults with ASDs begin seeing therapists because they are depressed and lonely. They've never had friends, and now don't know how to make/keep them. So your efforts to socialize a child shouldn't just be about what he wants, or even needs, *now*. Keep your eye on the long term. Your goal is for the child to become fluent enough in his social skills so that, as an adult, he'll be able to *choose* the level of social activity he wants in his life, rather than being isolated and without the ability to socially connect with others if he so desires.

Two Practical Considerations

As you work at providing regular, successful, enjoyable social experiences that can help the child master and generalize his social skills, you'll be confronted with two practical realities.

1. *You cannot control every social opportunity that the child experiences.* The social opportunities that are available depend somewhat on factors that are out of the control of parents or a school team. That includes the school administration's approach to social programming, the style of the classroom teacher, the availability of clubs and teams, and the number of same-age peers who live nearby. But, through your efforts you *can*
   - *create* social opportunities,
   - *adapt* existing social situations so the child can be successful,
   - *mobilize* the peer group to demonstrate better responses, and
   - *change the attitudes* of peers and adults.

2. *There are too many social skills, and they evolve too quickly, for us to provide a specific generalization plan for each.* Even if you targeted one social skill per month, that would only be 12 skills per year (and over the course of a year, the peer group's social skills would continue to develop, too, to the point that you would have to start over again the next year!).

The good news is that if you provide enough of the right social opportunities, a lot of social skills get generalized on their own. That means you should only have to specifically design generalization plans for some key skills. The more the child successfully participates in social activities and practices a range of social skills, the better he'll generalize a broad range of social competencies. Plus, the more he enjoys the social activities, the more motivated he'll be to improve his social interactions with his peers.

Summary

Generalization, or learning a skill in one setting or situation and being able to apply it in another, tends to be an area of weakness for children with ASDs. That's why, so often, you'll see children who perform beautifully during social skills class, but then fall apart out in the "real world."

If they're truly going to achieve their social skills goals, children with ASDs need to practice them in a range of progressively more difficult situations, with built-in supports that are gradually reduced as they no longer need them. These circumstances don't usually occur unless adults make the effort to organize them. That means, as the parent or teacher, it must become *your* goal to create social opportunities that: (a) occur regularly in the child's life, (b) facilitate successful interactions with his peers, (c) create a chance for him to practice social skills, and (d) are enjoyable for him. In the next chapter, we'll look at this objective in more specific terms, such as how to choose social opportunities, how to gauge their level of difficulty, and how much social participation you should expect.

Chapter 2

Identifying and Assessing Social Opportunities

- *How do you choose appropriate social opportunities?*

- *How much social activity is appropriate (and necessary)?*

- *How do you judge the difficulty of a particular social situation?*

As we discussed in Chapter 1, if a child on the spectrum is going to master and generalize the social skills he's being taught, he needs to practice them across different settings and with different people, every day. But you can't expect the child to do this on his own. You, as the adult, have to engineer the practice activities. The first step is putting together a calendar of appropriate social opportunities.

How Do You Choose Appropriate Social Opportunities?

When you're looking for opportunities for a child to practice his social skills, the best place to start is with the social opportunities that most children experience every day. Of course, these will vary somewhat, depending on several factors related to your community, family, and school. The point is to start by looking at where the child's peers typically interact with others. Later, we'll look at ways to make these opportunities accessible for your child.

Here are a few possibilities to consider.

At Home:
- ▶ Family meals
- ▶ Visits with relatives
- ▶ Sibling interactions
- ▶ Play dates
- ▶ Overnights/slumber parties

In the Community:
- ▶ Neighborhood peer gatherings
- ▶ Errands
- ▶ Sports teams (a child who's not comfortable playing might be able to participate as a manager or statistician)
- ▶ Martial arts or swimming lessons
- ▶ Music lessons
- ▶ Church/synagogue youth fellowship and activities
- ▶ Scouts

At School:
- ▶ Lunch
- ▶ Recess
- ▶ Study hall

- ▶ Specials: art, music, computer, tech ed, gym class
- ▶ Transitions between tasks in the classroom
- ▶ Hallway transitions/time at the locker
- ▶ Extracurricular clubs and teams
- ▶ Dances
- ▶ Field trips

When putting together a plan, be sure to consider the key social activities for your child's age group (see Table 2-1). These are the times when most children interact with their peers. Consequently, while these will not always present good chances for generalization, they are the situations in which you want the child to eventually be able to function independently.

Table 2-1

Key Social Opportunities	
Elementary School	**Middle and High School**
Lunch	Lunch
Recess	Hallways between classes
Play dates	Study hall/specials
Community-based clubs/teams	Extracurricular clubs/teams
Family occasions	Community-based clubs/teams

How Much Social Activity Is Appropriate (and Necessary)?

Once you've looked at what opportunities for social experiences are available, you need to figure out how frequently the child will participate in them. Remember, social interactions are essential if a child is going to improve his social skills. This applies even to the child who has little or no social motivation and actively avoids any social contact.

One effective way of addressing a child's reluctance is to build social practice into his preferred activities. For example, if he wants a new toy, don't just bring it home to him; insist that he go to the store and buy it (with appropriate levels of support). Or, if he wants to engage in certain activities (e.g., playing with Legos or video games), establish a rule that he has to do it for a certain length of time with peers, first. (We'll discuss using rewards and incentives to make social interaction more appealing in Chapter 3.)

The Child's Social Itinerary

As much as possible, build in *daily* social opportunities and target the most social times during the day. Just how much social practice is necessary and appropriate depends on the individual child, his skills, and his comfort with social situations.

The following itinerary would be a reasonable place to start for many children:
1. Social programming during part or all of lunch and recess, three to four days per week
2. One social occasion with a peer outside of school every two weeks
3. Participation in one school club or team
4. Participation in one community club or team

As the child shows progress, you can build in more frequent social opportunities. However, as we discuss below, it is very important not to overwhelm the child.

Monitoring Stress Levels

While it's natural for a child to experience a bit of anxiety about new social demands, be careful not to overwhelm him, leaving him stressed. You can monitor his stress level by watching for:
- behavior problems during and after social opportunities
- fatigue
- increased stimming or other regressive behaviors

If there are indications that the child is overwhelmed by the frequency of social demands placed on him, that's a sign that you should pull back. Not only will too much stress reduce a child's social motivation, it will reduce his ability to apply his social skills.

How Challenging Is a Particular Social Situation?

For children with ASDs, social situations fall on a continuum from easy to difficult, according to a number of criteria (e.g., Hudson & Coffin, 2007). Let's take a look at 10 of the most important factors contributing to the level of challenge (see Figure 2-1).

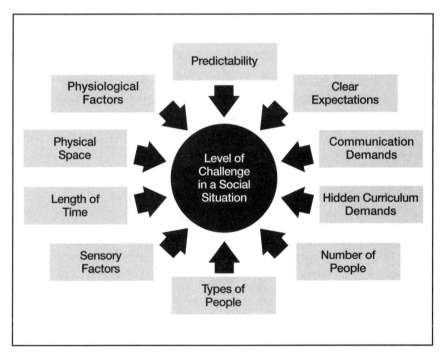

Figure 2-1: Factors Making Social Situations More Challenging

Predictability/Familiarity

The more familiar the situation is, and the more the child knows what is coming next, the easier it is for him to deal with. Most children on the spectrum love routines and repetitive events, because they reduce the need to analyze what is going on and predict what might happen next. That's why "circle time" at school, where the teacher goes through the same routine every day (sing the "Hello, Good Morning!" song; pass a greeting around the circle; raise your hand to share news; etc.) is much easier than a play date at a new friend's house, where you may not know what you're going to play, what you'll eat for a snack, or what your friend's mother is like.

Clarity of Expectations

For children with ASDs, it's a huge challenge to put together all the social information that is flying around them and figure out what to do – how to greet others, what to say, when to talk. Social situations are far easier when there are clear signs of what to do and when. That's why structured games are easier than "free play" time. You wait your turn, roll the dice, and move the correct number of squares. Or, you listen to a question, try to give an answer, and then go to the end of the line.

In contrast, a busy playground does not provide clear signs of what to do. Who do you approach? How do you join a game or a group activity? When can you talk to someone, yell, or sing? The social cues in this type of situation are more subtle and harder to follow. And as children grow into adolescents, the cues only become harder to read and the expectations, stricter.

Communication Demands

Communication skills pose challenges for all children on the spectrum. For some, the difficulties reach down to basic expressive and receptive language. Others (e.g., those with Asperger Syndrome or nonverbal learning disabilities) have higher-level struggles with conversation skills, figurative expressions, and subtle or abstract meanings.

Social situations are more difficult when there are greater communication demands. Compare going to church or temple with hanging out in the front yard with friends. For a child, going to a worship service typically means following your parents in, sitting quietly, and then returning home. The only communication requirement might be saying hello to people. "Hanging out," on the other hand, is tricky. You need to understand verbal and nonverbal communication, emotions, opinions, joking, and metaphors. So, the level of social challenge is much higher with peers in the neighborhood than going to a religious service.

Hidden Curriculum/Complexity of Social Conventions

The level of social challenge is also raised by the presence of implicit, but unstated, social conventions and routines known as the "hidden curriculum" (Myles, Trautman, & Schelvan, 2005). We are all surrounded by countless social rules that typical children pick up on their own or with some feedback from parents and others. This includes a wide range of rules (e.g., how to dress in given situations, who you can talk to in public, what to do when receiving a gift, where to stand on an elevator).

Situations that involve more unwritten rules present higher social demands because there are more things to think about and more ways to unwittingly offend or upset others. Supper at a fast-food restaurant is relatively easy in this regard. You wait in line, get your food, sit at the table, and eat (using reasonably acceptable table manners). In contrast, a dinner party is more difficult, as it involves many additional rules, such as how to dress, when it's okay to start eating, which fork or spoon to use, what's acceptable dinner conversation, and how loud you may talk.

Number of Participants

Another important dimension of social difficulty is the size of the group. Each person involved in an interaction adds more social information (verbal and nonverbal) to absorb and analyze, as well as another person who needs to understand what you say.

In general, the fewer people who are involved, the lower the social challenge. However, this is further complicated by group dynamics. In a one-to-one interaction, there is only one relationship to consider (e.g., child-to-parent, peer-to-peer, or student-to-teacher). In groups, another set of social behaviors is needed, depending on the roles and context of the participants. For example, we all act differently when we're alone with a friend than when we're with a group of coworkers or at a family gathering. There are subtle shifts in what we say and how we act in the more complex group situations.

Individuals Involved

Some people are easier to socialize with than others. This can be related to how they communicate. It's easier for a child on the spectrum to be social with people who speak slowly, listen carefully, articulate well, express themselves directly, minimize figurative language, and communicate their feelings through words as well as nonverbal channels, such as frowns and smiles.

But good communication skills aren't the only traits to look for. People who are patient, who genuinely *like* the child, and who send clear messages of affection and support, make social interaction much easier and more pleasant. Entertaining or funny people (as long as they don't mock others) are also less challenging social partners, because they're fun to be with.

Children with ASDs frequently prefer to interact with adults, rather than their peers. That's because adults are usually more tolerant and accepting of atypical behaviors and work harder at understanding and being understood. This greatly reduces the level of social challenge.

Sensory Demands

Many children with ASDs have nervous systems that process sensory information in unusual ways. They may experience some sensations too intensely and others not intensely enough. This may include sounds, sights, clothing textures, food textures, fragrances, temperature, or the general level of environmental stimulation.

The degree of social difficulty can dramatically increase if there are sensory challenges present. Participating in a predictable conversation with a familiar person can become difficult if it occurs in a noisy or highly active setting such as a shopping mall or a fair. Unfortunately, playgrounds and cafeterias, two of the most important social settings in schools, are notorious for being noisy, smelly, and active, which increases their social challenge.

Duration of the Social Activities

With any activity, the longer you do it, the more tired you get, and the more taxing it can become. Social processing is no different. A two-hour play date is far easier than spending an entire afternoon with a friend. Going out to a movie or getting a quick snack with friends and then going home presents a lower challenge level than a "sleepover" lasting 16 hours or more.

Physical Space

Spatial considerations can also be important in determining the level of social challenge. In general, crowded spaces or large, open areas present greater difficulty. Trying to interact with other people in a cramped setting can feel oppressive for a child, amplifying his sensory difficulties and making him lose his tentative grip on what's appropriate "personal space." On the other hand, wide-open space can be disorienting for some children, and for others can spur higher activity levels and a need to move around. The best spaces for practicing social skills are well-ordered with clear boundaries that provide enough space for the type of activity.

Child's Physiological State

Another key factor to take into consideration when gauging the level of social challenge is the condition of the child. Fatigue, hunger, thirst, or illness can make social challenges extremely difficult, and can turn what would usually be an easy situation into a really difficult one. No one feels as sociable when they're not feeling well. For a child with an ASD, social processing requires focus, concentration, and a balanced energy level. When he's feeling under the weather, his social performance will suffer, and the level of challenge will rise.

Ten Questions to Ask When Assessing a Social Situation's Potential Difficulty

1. How many times has the child been in the situation before? Does he know what to expect?

2. Are you clearly letting him know what is expected of him?

3. What communication skills will he have to use?

4. Are there a lot of unwritten rules that need to be followed?

5. How many other people will be there?

6. Is it easy to interact with the people who will be there?

7. How noisy, visually stimulating, and generally chaotic will it be? Can he handle the sensory challenges?

8. How long will the activity last?

9. Does the setting fit the activity?

10. Is he tired, hungry, or sick?

Choosing and Assessing Opportunities

The 10 factors we've just discussed are all important, but you can't apply them in a generic way. No two children are exactly alike, and each dimension will play out differently for each child and each situation (Hudson & Coffin, 2007). That means that you'll need to judge a particular activity's level of social challenge on a case-by-case basis for each child. Even then, don't expect every opportunity you choose to be perfect right out of the gate. Plan on starting slowly and making adjustments as you go.

Children on the spectrum often have fight-or-flight reactions to situations that overwhelm them, so you always want to ease them gently into more social activity. Start out with opportunities that have a relatively low level of challenge for the child, and then gradually raise the level of difficulty as he can handle it.

How do you judge his handling of a social situation? There are four indicators to look at: level of enjoyment, performance of social skills, presence of problem behaviors, and indicators of excessive stress.

Enjoyment

The easiest – and often the best – barometer of a situation is *whether the child is having a good time*. If the child complains about an activity and tries to avoid it, those are indicators that adjustments are needed. This may include reducing the level of challenge or adding supports (see Chapter 3).

Performance

A social opportunity should be fun for a child, but for kids with ASDs, enjoyment doesn't always equate to social interaction. Therefore, it's important to look at what social skills the child is practicing. If he is isolating himself or doing more observing than interacting, the situation may need to be adjusted downward. Alternately, if the child is very comfortable in the situation and can manage it just fine without actually having to *use* the higher end of his social skills, then he needs more challenge.

Behavior Problems

Negative or disruptive behaviors are a child's way of communicating a problem. When a child is unable to express in words that a social opportunity is too difficult or too boring, he may make it clear through tantrums or other disruptive behaviors that lead to his being removed from the situation. Obviously, such behaviors indicate that the social opportunity, as it stands, is not appropriate. Either the difficulty level needs to be changed or supports need to be added.

Stress Reactions

In some cases, the child may enjoy and participate well in a situation but then break down afterward, exhibiting tantrums or angry behavior. He may complain of headaches or show signs of fatigue (e.g., tired appearance, irritability, falling asleep during activities or in the car). These stress reactions may be telling you that even though the child may be enjoying the social opportunity, the demands are taking too great a toll on his skills and leaving him experiencing significant stress. When such stress indications are present, you should review the social opportunity and consider making adjustments.

Table 2-2 presents a checklist of questions to ask when assessing a situation. If the answer to most or all of these questions is "yes," then the situation is probably working well for the child. However, if there are more than a few "nos," you may need to change one or more dimensions of difficulty (e.g., reduce the duration), add or reduce supports (see Chapter 3), or decide to stop having the child participate in the activity altogether.

Table 2-2

	Situational Assessment Checklist
Enjoyment	☐ Does he enjoy participating in the situation? ☐ Does he ask to participate or seem disappointed when it is cancelled? ☐ Is he upset when it is time to end?
Performance	☐ Is he practicing some easier social skills without difficulty? ☐ Is he practicing some more difficult social skills and receiving the supports he needs to be successful?
Behavior Problems	☐ Does he control himself and avoid exhibiting any persistent behavior problems just before or during the activity?
Stress Reactions	☐ Does he manage the situation without getting tired out? ☐ Does he do well in meeting the demands of the activities that follow the situation? ☐ Does he mind you without difficulty after the situation ends? ☐ Does he maintain self-control and avoid demonstrating tantrums or other problem behavior afterwards?

Summary

When putting together a schedule of social activities for a child with an ASD, it's helpful to start by looking at *all* the social situations in his life and deciding which are the most important and which provide the best opportunities to practice social skills. Children should be expected to participate in regular social activities so they experience them often enough to get comfortable in them and master the social skills that they need.

Social situations vary in difficulty for each child depending on a number of factors, including the type of expectations placed on him, the predictability and familiarity of the situation, and the number of people who are present. The challenge for parents and school teams is to ensure that the child is participating in enough social situations that are at the appropriate level of challenge. Because optimal situations aren't always available, in the next chapter, we'll look at ways to adapt the level of difficulty in a social situation.

Chapter 3

Ensuring Success in Social Activities

- *Setting up optimal social situations*
- *Supports and strategies for any situation*
  - *Teaching the situation*
  - *Tools*
  - *Incentives and rewards*
  - *Peer mentors and adult interventions*
- *Measuring progress*
- *Withdrawing supports*

In Chapter 2, we discussed choosing social situations and assessing their level of difficulty. Building on that, let's take a look at how you can adapt those situations for the child, and how you can tell if your efforts are working.

The key to helping a child generalize his social skills is providing plenty of practice opportunities that are both fun and appropriately challenging – neither too easy nor too stressful. Some you can set up yourself, which allows you to build in an optimal amount of challenge. Of course, for most social situations, you won't have that much control, but you can still adjust their level of difficulty using a variety of tools and strategies.

When You're in Charge: Setting up the Situation

In situations where you have control (e.g., setting up a play date at your house or organizing a group activity at school), you can adjust all 10 of the dimensions of difficulty we discussed in Chapter 2.

- ▶ **Familiarity/Predictability:** Set up a predictable and familiar schedule of activities.
- ▶ **Clear Expectations:** Use a lot of games or structured conversations where the expectations are clear.
- ▶ **Communication Demands:** Choose activities that entail minimal demands for higher levels of communication skills.
- ▶ **Hidden Curriculum:** Minimize the number of social conventions and unwritten rules that must be followed.
- ▶ **Participants:** Include the right number of people and invite only ones the child is familiar with and finds easy to talk to.
- ▶ **Sensory Demands:** Manage the noise level, degree of activity, exposure to foods, tactile inputs, or fragrances.
- ▶ **Duration and Setting:** Keep the activity short and conduct it in a well-controlled and appropriate space.
- ▶ **Physiological Status:** Ensure that the child has eaten and is well rested before starting.

Table 3-1 presents sample plans for three social activities with different levels of challenge. In each case, the parents carefully assessed the level of difficulty and ensured that the challenges presented were at an appropriate level for their child. It is important to remember that the goal is not to make it as easy as possible, but to prevent the challenges from overwhelming the child and to present a level of difficulty that allows the child to practice and apply his social skills.

Table 3-1

	Least Challenging: *Playing Board Games at Home*	More Challenging: *Picnicking and Playing in the Park*	Most Challenging: *Attending a Big Sporting Event in a Nearby City*
Dimensions of Difficulty for Three Social Activities for an 8- to 12-Year-Old Boy			
Familiarity/ Predictability	Games are well known and practiced	Park setting, foods, and play activities are familiar, but not everyday events	Activities are unfamiliar: long car ride with friends, walking in the city, being in a stadium
Clarity of Expectations	Clear expectations for behavior (child knows what to do and how to do it)	More subtle expectations related to what to play, when to eat, and where to go	Many unclear expectations, such as length of ride, length of game, how and when to cheer
Communication Demands	Limited unstructured conversation	Periods of conversation during play	Extended periods of conversation in the car and during the game; use of sports jargon
Hidden Curriculum	Few unwritten rules	Some unwritten rules and expectations for playground activities and pretend play	Varying rules for acceptable behavior in the car, in a restaurant, at the game, and in public restrooms
Number of Participants	One or two peers	Three or four peers	Four peers
Individuals Involved	Well-known, "nice" students from school	Familiar peers from the neighborhood	Peers from the sports team (including some the child doesn't know well)
Sensory Demands	Well controlled in the home	Noise, sunlight, outdoor temperature, sand/grass, food textures may create problems	Noise at the game, odors in the city, exposure to crowds all may be problematic
Duration	1 to 2 hours	2 to 3 hours	Travel and game, 4 to 5 hours
Setting	Appropriately sized room with necessary table and chairs	Well-equipped park with playground and picnic tables	Crowded car, city streets, enormous stadium
Physiological Status	Child is well fed and rested; snack is provided during game	Child is fed, but may be tired from play	Child may experience difficulties with hunger and thirst during car ride; long day can be exhausting

Ensuring Success in Social Activities • 31

Tools and Strategies for Any Situation

In situations where you aren't the one making the plans and the invitations, you may have little or no control over the dimensions of difficulty. On the playground, in the hallways, or in the neighborhood, you may only be able to control the duration of the activity. When that's the case, you'll need to turn to other strategies, tools, and supports to make the activity a better social opportunity for the child.

Teaching the Situation

The best way to address the challenges of familiarity/predictability and clarity of expectations is to *teach the situation* to the child: To make ...

the unfamiliar → familiar

the unpredictable → predictable

unclear expectations → clear

Children with autism or other developmental disabilities can often master a situation if they are given the necessary information in a format that allows them to learn it (Hudson & Coffin, 2007). The most popular ways of teaching the situation include briefing the child beforehand on what to expect ("priming") and debriefing him afterward to review what went well and what was difficult. The latter is often called a "social autopsy" (e.g., Myles & Southwick, 2005).

For some children, talking through the situation may be all it takes. Tell them:

- ► What will happen (in terms that they can understand and remember)
- ► What will be expected of them (what to do and when)
- ► Who will be there and how they will probably behave
- ► What problems might occur and what strategies they should use if they do
- ► What the relevant hidden curriculum rules are

For a child and/or situation that requires a more concerted effort, the key is to provide the information in a format that enables him to remember it and use it. For many children, using Social Stories™ (Gray & White, 2002), comic strip conversations (Gray, 1994), or written or picture scripts is effective. For others, it may be necessary to role play what will happen and how they can successfully respond.

This type of instruction can greatly reduce the level of social challenge and can turn an overwhelming situation into a successful one. Of course, it isn't possible – or necessary – to teach every possible challenging social situation. Teaching should be reserved for opportunities where inclusion is important (e.g., frequent social situations such as the playground and cafeteria), or situations where problems seem to regularly occur.

Tools

A variety of tools can help make a social situation less challenging for a child. Some arm him with information he'll need to maneuver a situation. Others help with self-regulation when circumstances may be anxiety provoking.

Informational tools. Informational tools give the child easy access to the key facts he'll need to meet the social demands of the situation. There is a wide range of possibilities here (see Gagnon, 2001; Hodgdon, 1995; Quill, 2000).

Rule Cards spell out essential behaviors to exhibit or guidelines to follow (e.g., "Power Cards," Gagnon, 2001). For example, they can provide reminders about:
- **proper greeting behaviors:** *Make eye contact. Shake hands. Say, "Hello, it's nice to meet you."*
- **problematic behaviors to avoid:** *Do Not: 1. Pick nose, 2. Put fingers in mouth, 3. Give bear hugs.*

▶ **play rules:** *1. Let Joey choose the first game, 2. Share toys with him, 3. Say "Nice game" when he wins.*

Rule cards should be customized to fit the child. Most children with ASDs like the structure that explicit rules provide. Moreover, they take in and process visual information more easily than verbal instruction. As a result, rule cards can help them effectively manage social situations that are otherwise daunting.

Conversation Starters are cards with appropriate topics listed on them that the child can carry with him (e.g., Quill, 2000). Often, one of the biggest obstacles to social interaction is not knowing what to talk about, especially when initiating a conversation. This type of card provides a ready reference to consult when confronted with a conversational opportunity, as illustrated below.

Things to Talk About

1. Yesterday's snowstorm.

2. The joke about the horse that Dad told you.

3. The baseball game on television last night.

Scripts provide even more help than conversation starters and can be helpful for children who are learning to use greetings and make small talk (e.g., Freeman & Dake, 1997). While scripts limit the spontaneity of a conversation, they can allow a child enough comfort to engage in beginning forms of conversational turn-taking. With a script, the child can focus on the other person and the problem of when to speak, instead of having to generate content.

Scripts generally require you to have a person who has been coached and knows how to respond. For example, for Marty, a middle school student, the team prepared several familiar peers to stop him in the hall and engage with him. Marty had a script to follow.

Marty's Script
– Hi (peer's name). How are you?
– Did you see (television show) last night?
– What did you think was funny?
– I liked it when everybody fell into the swimming pool.

Each peer answered Marty's questions and then asked several questions of his own (for which Marty was prepared).

Situational Fact Sheets (Hodgdon, 1995) are brief descriptions providing key information pertaining to a difficult situation. In essence, they are easy-to-read summaries of the information you have already taught the child about an upcoming event. They tell him what's going to happen, when, with whom, and what to look for. They may also include a checklist or score sheet for the child to mark off things as he sees or does them.

A good example of this tool was used with Toby, an elementary school child who had to attend a family reunion. The situational fact sheet listed the key people who would be there, the schedule of events, key rules to follow (e.g., *Say hello and shake hands when meeting new people*), and a map of the park grounds where the party was being held. With this visual tool, Toby was able to tolerate the event for over two hours, and he even enjoyed himself.

Informational tools are invaluable for many children. The key is to individualize them so they capture key information in a format that the child can understand. Tools don't have to be written; they can be based on pictures. As Gagnon (2001) emphasizes, you can enhance their effectiveness by including content that is interesting to the child. One parent I know made extensive use of rule cards over many years with pictures of *Peanuts* characters, which were the child's passion.

Relaxers/fidgets. This set of tools helps with self-regulation. Social situations can be anxiety provoking, especially when they take place in noisy, active settings that make sensory processing more difficult. When this is the case, it can be worthwhile to give the child "fidgets" or toys that will allow him to stay calm and prevent over-arousal. Items such as theraputty, a "Koosh" ball, rubber tubing, an action figure, or relaxing pictures help some children stay focused and self-regulate in challenging social situations.

Choose a fidget carefully, with the individual child in mind. Then coach him on how to use it in a way that doesn't draw negative attention or bother people. A fidget that the child finds *too* fun or interesting can over-stimulate or distract him, rather than support his social functioning.

Jacob

One elementary school student I knew, Jacob, benefited at first from having a Koosh ball to squeeze during classes. It calmed him down and helped him to pay attention. Unfortunately, he developed the habit of holding one of fibers on the Koosh and twirling it. When it slipped out of his hand (which it did on a regular basis), it would fly across the room, landing on other students' desks and distracting everyone. Needless to say, we needed to find a different fidget!

Environmental supports. Some children do well with tools that help to structure the environment for them. For example, schedules and visual timers can help a child gauge how long he'll have to endure a difficult situation. Without these tools, it may feel to him as if the social discomfort will go on forever, and this can spark negative or disruptive behaviors. In the same way, maps or diagrams of a building can help the setting feel more predictable to the child, which in turn can help him remain settled enough to engage in social interactions.

Kenny

*Kenny was resistant to having play dates where he had
to interact with a peer. His mother solved this by setting
up a visual timer and negotiating a deal with him where,
once he played with the peer for 20 minutes, he could
play video games for 10 minutes. Kenny quickly learned
to tolerate play dates once Mom put this combination of
environmental structure and incentive into place.*

Incentives/Rewards as Reinforcers

As we discussed in Chapter 1, some children with ASDs don't
find socializing intrinsically rewarding, especially at first. When
this is the case, you have to address motivation. Offering an incentive or reward to the child for using certain social skills or tol-
erating a situation for a certain length of time can help him pay
attention to his behavior and exert more effort at being social.

That doesn't mean you have to bust your budget at the toy store.
Rewards can be as simple as taking him for fries at his favorite
fast-food restaurant, allowing him a few minutes extra time with
his favorite video game, or letting him stay up past his normal
bedtime. *The key is to assess the child's preferences to make certain that the incentive will really be motivating for him.*

When using reinforcers, it is important to keep it very positive. You
want the child to willingly engage in a social interaction, because
he finds it rewarding in some way. Avoid using consequences or
punishments. If the child associates social demands with negative
experiences, it will backfire on you: He'll become less motivated to
engage in social experiences and less compliant with your requests.

You also want to make sure that you don't offer rewards for a
behavior that the child isn't able to perform or a situation that he

can't handle. That's not motivation. That's setting a child up for failure, and he'll likely respond with frustration and anger.

Peer Mentors and Adult Intervention

Whatever the difficulty level of a given situation, assistance from trained, supportive peers or adults can help a child negotiate the social labyrinth. A peer mentor is a more naturally occurring type of support; while adult intervention will change the nature of the social situation (with the adult's presence), it allows for more skilled and intrusive help to the child.

Peer Mentors

The guidance and support offered by a trained peer can substantially reduce the level of challenge in a situation and make a potentially uncomfortable social opportunity enjoyable for a child. The role of a peer mentor is very flexible and, depending on the individuals and the circumstances, can range from just providing a supportive presence to prompting the child to perform certain appropriate social behaviors (or stop performing inappropriate ones).

When setting up a peer mentorship program, it's important that you not only choose students with the right characteristics, but that you also provide appropriate structure, training, and monitoring. Peer mentoring will be discussed in detail in Chapter 6.

Adult Intervention

The most powerful way to change the difficulty level of a social opportunity is through the intervention of school staff, parents, or other adults. Yet, this method exacts the greatest price with regard to the child's independence, as it's the most difficult to withdraw when the child no longer needs it. Adult interventions are introduced here, but will be discussed at greater length in Chapter 5.

It can be helpful to think about adults providing support at three distinct levels, from least to most intrusive.

- ▶ **Monitor level.** The least intrusive level consists of just monitoring the situation from a distance. The adult is there to rescue the child if significant problems occur, such as teasing, disruptive behaviors, or irresolvable conflict.

- ▶ **Guide level.** Here the adult stays close to the action and provides information to the child – predicting what is going to happen, explaining what people are saying (through words or nonverbal means), and prompting the child to keep him involved and responding at appropriate times. At this level, the adult is clearly present in the interaction, but she attends and communicates only with the child, acting as a guide.

- ▶ **Intervention level.** At this, the most intrusive level, the adult goes beyond being a guide and intervenes with all the peers participating in the interaction. She may recruit peers to interact with the child, set up a game or a structured conversation, direct the peers in how to respond to the child, and prompt all the children as they converse.

The objective for the adult is to be as non-intrusive as possible, yet to provide enough support to ensure a successful interaction. The more active a role the adult takes, the less challenging the situation is for the child, and the more difficult it will be to later withdraw the support. Adult supports and interventions will be discussed in more detail in Chapter 5.

Measuring Progress

If you're going to make the effort to put interventions and supports into place for a child, also make sure you have a method in place for assessing their effectiveness. The objective of all these efforts is to help the child improve his use of appropriate social skills. Measuring progress with this objective is essential to ensuring that you are on the right track, that your efforts are successful, and that you can justify the resources going into your efforts.

Measuring social behavior is a difficult but important component of any program (e.g., Bellini, 2006). It's especially tricky with children, because children are constantly developing and, therefore, constantly changing. In addition, the "standard" for social behavior is also changing as they get older. For example, conversation skills for a third grader are different from those of a fourth or fifth grader. There is no distinct set of target skills to master for each age. Rather, competencies continue to evolve and to be performed at more advanced levels. This is more difficult to reliably track.

Because this program focuses not on teaching specific social skills, but on providing opportunities for a child to practice and generalize them, what you'll want to measure is *the extent to which the child is advancing in his demonstration of social skills during social opportunities.*

There are three general ways to assess progress. These vary in the amount of time they require and, generally, "you get what you pay for" in terms of effort. While it is easiest to just ask people how they think the child is doing, that doesn't always give you the most accurate assessment or the detailed information you need to determine next steps.

Informal Assessment

Informal assessment is the easiest and fastest method to use, and therefore the most common. Through discussion at team meetings or between teachers and parents, people state their sense of how the child is coming with his social skills. These general views are then translated into goals and objectives for the IEP once a year.

Unfortunately, these assessments are vulnerable to being inaccurate and imprecise. They may be unduly influenced by certain situations that are particularly memorable (e.g., the one great day Billy asked another boy to play catch, or the really bad day when Terri hit another girl in the head with the toy teapot). Or the reports may come from people who do not see the child's social interactions up close. For example, in one team meeting, the principal confidently asserted that Ann was showing great improvement in social skills. She had learned this from the speech therapist, who was seeing significant gains during individual and group speech sessions. However, the teacher and the aide had a very different report – the child was not generalizing those improvements outside the speech therapy room. She continued to be isolated in the classroom and on the playground during recess.

While never a "perfect" measure, there are ways to improve informal assessments. For example, it can help to:

- ▶ have regular meetings (e.g., monthly) where you systematically get input from the same people each time,
- ▶ use a standard set of questions (e.g., Bellini, 2006), and
- ▶ have people indicate *when* and *where* they were able to observe the child's social behaviors.

Questionnaires and Rating Scales

Questionnaires and rating scales may be used to more systematically rate the child's progress (see Bellini, 2006). While these instruments are still vulnerable to subjective bias, they are much more dependable than informal reports. It's important to choose the right instrument and to keep the ratings as specific as possible. You want to use the instrument that best addresses the behaviors with which you are concerned.

Some questionnaires address general social skills (e.g., *Social Skills Rating System*, Gresham & Elliott, 1990; *School Social Behavior Scales,* Merrell, 2002), and some look at more autism-specific social challenges (e.g., *Assessment of Social and Communication Skills for Children with Autism*, Quill, 2000; *Autism Social Skills Profile*, Bellini, in press). However, these are generally not sensitive enough to pick up changes over the short run or to monitor improvement on a day-to-day basis.

Observational Ratings

The best (and most rigorous) way to measure progress is to observe the child in social settings and to systematically record key behaviors. This is not as difficult as it sounds. This type of effort can be guided by a school psychologist or an autism consultant who has experience with observational data. With minimal training, parents and school staff (including teachers, aides, or specialists) can collect reliable data on a child's social performance.

Observations should target the most social times during the day (see Table 3-2), and should be done multiple times, each long enough to get a valid sample of the child's behavior. (Watching a child for 10 minutes is not sufficient.) A single observation, even one lasting one to two hours, is suspect as well, because the child could be having an unusually good or bad day. On the other hand, four to six half-hour observations during key times can capture the child's functioning with some confidence. Observers should be careful to rate behaviors that they can accurately see and reliably judge. Counting the number of peer interactions or the number of times a child initiated social contact is straightforward and easily measured. Rating eye contact, voice tone, or conversational content can be more difficult and will require more practice to ensure that the ratings are accurate and reliable.

Table 3-2

| Good Situations for Observational Ratings ||
Elementary School	Middle and High School
Recess	Lunch
Lunch	Hallways between classes
Morning work	Study hall
Group learning activities	Extracurricular activities
Gym class	Group learning activities

Matthew

Matthew was a fourth grader with a diagnosis of Asperger Syndrome. In order to track his social progress, the team trained his aide to take observational data during recess and his "free work" period (a less structured and more social time in the classroom). The aide made observations for two-week periods, five times over the course of the school year. During each two-week period, she did three to four hours of observation. She was trained to track the frequency of peer interactions and to note whether or not Matthew used appropriate eye contact.

The results are presented in Figures 3-1 and 3-2. They clearly showed progress and confirmed that the team's program was on target. His interactions became more frequent (e.g., at recess, he went from 18 to 28 peer interactions per hour) and his appropriate eye contact increased from approximately two-thirds of the time to almost 100% of the time.

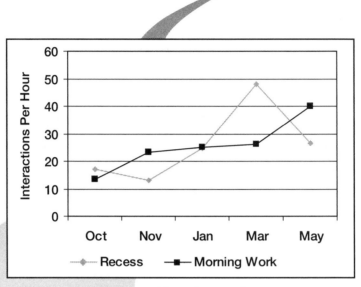

Figure 3-1: Frequency of Peer Interactions

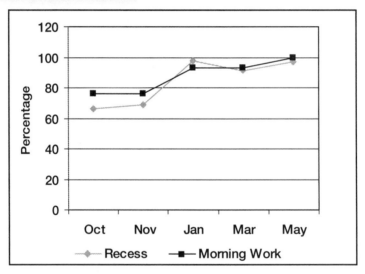

Figure 3-2: Percentage of Interactions with Appropriate Eye Contact

Observational measurement is a valuable tool. The social behavior of children and adolescents is complex and ever changing and, therefore, is hard to capture with questionnaires or rating scales. Watching the child in social situations and noting even the most basic social indices (e.g., number of initiations during recess, percentage of positive and negative peer responses) gives you an effective report card on social functioning that can let you know the success of your efforts and guide your program planning. It does require some staff time (e.g., 16-20 hours of an aide's time over the course of a school year) and a systematic approach to scheduling observations and compiling the data, but it's worth the effort in terms of accurate, useable data.

Withdrawing Supports

Whenever you put supports into a social situation, you must also think about how you'll eventually withdraw them. Instead of abruptly withdrawing a support, you need to gradually reduce its use as the child masters a situation and applies his skills more and more independently. Let's take a look at how we could do this with each type of support we've discussed.

Teaching the Situation: Fading Strategies

Teaching strategies can be gradually withdrawn in several ways: (a) The *amount* of information being taught or reviewed can be gradually reduced; (b) the *length* of teaching sessions can be shortened; or (c) the *frequency* of teaching sessions can be reduced.

You can use one or more withdrawal strategies for any given support. In the following example, Zoey had become much more independent and comfortable talking with other girls at the lunch table, so her teacher used all three methods to gradually decrease her lunchtime Social Stories™:
1. Initially, reviewed Social Stories for 15 minutes every morning before lunch.
2. Reviewed Social Stories for 5 minutes every morning before lunch. *(Reduced length)*

3. Reviewed Social Stories for 5 minutes on Monday, Wednesday, and Friday. *(Reduced frequency)*
4. Moved from Social Stories to a list of three rules to follow; reviewed for 5 minutes on Monday, Wednesday, and Friday. *(Reduced amount of information)*
5. Reviewed three rules for 5 minutes on Tuesday and Thursday. *(Reduced frequency)*
6. Reviewed three rules once a week. *(Reduced frequency)*
7. Discontinued review of the rules.

For Zoey, each of these steps took about two weeks, but it is hard to predict: Some children might need more time, and some a lot less. The key is to try to move forward a step and see if the child continues to be successful. If not, return to the previous step for more time.

Phasing out Tools

The process of gradually reducing the use of informational tools, relaxers/fidgets, and environmental supports generally occurs in three phases. In the first and standard condition, the adult determines when and for how long the child needs the tool. In the second stage, you hand control of the tool over to the child, letting him decide when he needs it. Typically, the child will use the tool less and less frequently until he reaches the third phase, where he no longer uses or needs it. Of course, sometimes a child in the second stage won't use the tool when he needs it. If that happens, move him back to the first stage while you provide more teaching and rehearsal with the tool or offer a specific reinforcer when he uses it.

Withdrawing Adult Interventions

Adult supports and interventions are the most difficult to fade out (see Chapter 5). In general terms, the process is moving from Intervention Level to Guide Level to Monitor Level. When considering moving from one level to the next, the criterion is: What does the child need to successfully participate in social interactions? For example, at recess, if the child isolates himself when left to his own devices, then Intervention Level interventions (e.g., recruiting peers, structuring games) are still needed. However, if the child can approach peers, engages with them, and maintains interactions, then the aide can move to Guide Level or even Monitor Level.

One of the reasons why fading adult intervention is so difficult is that children with ASDs often struggle with "prompt dependency" (e.g., Quill, 2000), meaning that they learn to associate the desired behavior with a specific cue from an adult, rather than the situation. For example, a child may learn to greet others whenever a staff member tells him "Say hi," but never do so without the verbal reminder. The process of fading prompts usually entails moving along a "prompt hierarchy" from higher to lower levels, such as in Table 3-4.

Carl

Once when observing a middle school student, Carl, I watched him walk down a busy hallway between classes. He approached his locker and then just stood there, facing it, for 3 minutes. Finally, an aide walked up and made eye contact with him. At this point, Carl put in the combination to the lock, opened the door, put some books away, took some other books out, closed the locker, and proceeded to his next class.

*Carl had mastered all the skills needed to appropriately
make the transition to his next class, but he was dependent on the visual cue of the aide in order to proceed.
The team had done a great job of teaching Carl the
skills necessary to carry out a difficult transition, but
had not completed the final step of teaching him how to
apply the skills without a prompt from staff.*

Table 3-4

	Sample Hierarchy of Prompts
(Highest)	Physical prompts: Physically guiding or orienting the child to initiate or maintain interactions (e.g., putting your arm around him and guiding him to the proximity of a peer)
	Verbal prompts: Verbally directing or reminding the child of what to do in social interactions (e.g., "Remember to greet Billy," "Make eye contact")
	Visual prompts: Using gestures, eye contact, or cards to remind the child to exhibit a key behavior (e.g., make eye contact with the child and touch your nose to cue him to stop picking his nose)
	Use of tool: Providing a rule card that the child can consult when uncertain (e.g., Greeting tips: 1. Make eye contact, 2. Shake hands, 3. Say "Hello")
(Lowest)	No prompts or tools: Independent functioning by the child

Withdrawing Incentives and Rewards

When it's time to start withdrawing supports and interventions, it's essential that you encourage the student to apply his skills more and more independently. Some children do well if supports are gradually reduced without any external motivators, but most children with ASDs still need positive feedback and/or incentives to persist during this challenging period. The key is to gradually "raise the bar" by tying rewards to increasingly independent social performance.

Let's look at verbal praise, the easiest and most direct form of encouragement. Verbal praise can vary in intensity, from "Way to go! That was awesome!" to just a simple "Nice." At first, you want to reward successful participation with *full support* with the most exuberant verbal praise. As time goes on, you adjust the standard so that you reserve the strongest verbal praise for successful participation with *less support*. This continues until the strongest verbal praise is reserved for *completely independent* performance.

For example, Larry, a 10-year-old, initially received strong verbal feedback for greeting a peer with physical and verbal prompts from his aide. As he became more comfortable with this, he received less exuberant praise when receiving the help, but more intense positive feedback when he approached the peer by himself or when he completed the greeting without any prompts.

Summary

There are many ways in which parents and school team members can adjust the difficulty level of a social situation. You can set up the situation (when you have that control), teach the situation to the child ahead of time, give him tools to help him function in the situation, train peer mentors, and/or provide adult interventions. These are all valuable ways to create a range of appropriate social opportunities. However, you want to also be sure that you measure the child's progress, and systematically remove supports as they become unnecessary, so that the child does not become dependent on them.

In the next four chapters, we will look in detail at the main vehicles used to create social opportunities: group interventions, adult interventions, peer mentors, and extracurricular activities.

Chapter 4

Using Groups to Provide Social Opportunities

- *Setting up a group-based intervention*
- *Key considerations*
- *Examples of successful groups*

The most common approach to promoting social skills is through group-based interventions. These are adult-structured social activities where children with ASDs can practice their social skills with typical peers. There are many different ways to do this. You can hold these sessions in the general education classroom, in the resource room, or in the office of a psychologist, social worker, or speech therapist. You can have the children play structured games and activities or just engage in casual conversation. The focus is on creating opportunities that encourage interaction and sharing.

These social practice opportunities are different from social skills *training* groups. It's usually best to *teach* new social skills in a separate setting, where you can discuss the children's challenges and give them feedback about their performance without an audience of typical peers (some of whom might tease or stigmatize the child).

You can create social practice opportunities with either segregated or integrated groups, but try to limit direct and individualized teaching when there are typical peers present.

One of the most popular group-based interventions is the Lunch Bunch (e.g., Wagner, 1999). Cafeterias are notoriously noisy and active and, therefore, can overwhelm the sensory processing of students with ASDs. Still, lunch is typically a very social time for kids, so it's important for them to interact with others during this daily occasion. The solution is to take the student with an ASD and a small group of his peers out of the cafeteria and have them eat lunch together in a separate, quieter room with staff present to facilitate conversation.

The basic principles of the Lunch Bunch can be applied when organizing any group-based intervention:

- ▶ Establish a setting where the student can successfully interact.
- ▶ Recruit supportive peers who will engage with him.
- ▶ Provide an activity that promotes interaction and conversation.
- ▶ Include an appropriate level of staff facilitation (see Chapter 5 for a discussion of adult supports and interventions).

When you're looking for ways to help a child generalize his social skills, there are several advantages to group-based interventions.

As the adult in charge, you can exert a relatively high level of control. For example, you can (a) build in predictability and routine, (b) adjust the sensory environment, (c) set clear expectations for what to do and when to do it, (d) put time limits on the activity, (e) handpick the group members, and (f) make sure that the social demands and environmental challenges are neither too low nor too high. And, in most situations, you'll also be able to keep the group fairly private, protecting the child from the scrutiny of the peer group at large, so he won't later be teased or targeted for things he's said or done.

Such control comes with a price. Group-based interventions are generally less like the natural environment and, therefore, provide a smaller step toward full generalization than social activities in a less structured and more natural situation. However, they are a very useful first-step intervention for many students.

Setting up a Group-Based Intervention

There are several important parameters to consider when designing a group-based intervention, including the following.

Who

Most group-based interventions include same-age peers. As we discussed in Chapter 1, same-age peers can be the most challenging in terms of social interaction, but offer the best opportunities for friendship and intimacy. How many peers you should include depends on the level and type of skills the child needs to practice. Using just one or two peers would allow for easier conversation and more attention to the student with the ASD. A larger group would present more challenge, because the child would need to track verbal and nonverbal information from several people at once.

When forming a group, you must consider not just the size of the group, but also the composition. It's okay to include more than one student with special needs, but at least half the group should be made up of typical classmates, so the child is learning to generalize his social skills with a range of peers. It's also important to consider compatibility. How do the children get along? Do they even like each other? The wrong combination will lead to an emphasis on conflict resolution and behavior management instead of positive social skills practice. It's not unusual to find group situations where animosity between two members leads to repeated insults and hurtful comments. There are also groups where staff have attempted to mix children with ASDs with other students who have anger management or antisocial behavior issues. Problems like these can disrupt the goals of the group.

When

Group-based interventions are usually conducted during social times outside the academic schedule, particularly during lunch, recess, study hall, flex periods, or after school. The duration of the activity is generally determined by the length of the class or lunch period. An ideal length of time is 45 to 60 minutes. Because of their difficulties with transitions, children with ASDs require some time to settle in at the beginning and to prepare to leave at the end of a session. In addition, for some, eating and talking at the same time is too challenging, so the interactive part of the group can only start after lunch is eaten. Considering all these factors, a 30- or 45-minute period should still allow a nice, if brief, social opportunity. At the same time, trying to insert a social practice event into a 20-minute lunch period is unrealistic.

Students with ASDs generally do better in repetitive, predictable situations, so sessions should be scheduled on a regular basis – at least weekly. True, that can be tricky. Sometimes it seems like school routines are constantly being interrupted by vacation and early dismissal days, assemblies, field trips, and testing. But there's no getting around the fact that it is much more difficult for students to productively use these activities if they occur infrequently or on an unpredictable basis.

Where

Group interventions usually take place in a separate office or classroom. They can also be done in the elementary classroom during center-based instruction, on the playground, or on a community trip. In cases where there is a risk that a stigma will be attached to the group, it is important to hold it in a location where students will be comfortable attending. Consequently, in some cases, the school psychologist's office may be less preferable than an administrative meeting room in the main office or one of the guidance department rooms.

Recruiting Participants

Typically, staff members identify and recruit kids to participate in the group. In some elementary school models, the student with the ASD chooses who will come with him. This works well when the activity is seen as a desirable privilege, but can backfire if peers lose interest in coming to the activity and the student is put in the uncomfortable situation of being turned down by most of the students he asks.

Some interventions rotate groups of students through the group. This can be a good way to involve a wider range of peers. But it's also important to make sure that the turnover isn't so rapid that it undermines the ability of the student with special needs to relate to the other participants.

When starting out, see if there are any naturally occurring groups of peers who already have connections to the student or know him from past years. For example, Albert, a middle school student, had a large extended family living in his town, so the school team drew on his cousins and family friends when recruiting.

Because the groups are generally highly structured with staff present, you should only need to provide minimal training of the typical peers. If the child with special needs presents disruptive or anxiety-provoking behaviors, it is helpful to explain the behavior and give the other children ways to respond (e.g., saying "quiet hands" or folding their hands in front of them to give a visual cue).

Choice of Activities

The activity itself should be social and enjoyable. Keep away from games like chess or gin rummy that require a high focus on strategy, because they can lead to intense competition without much social interaction. Instead, choose games that require social interaction. This can include word games such as *Password*, *The Match Game*, or *Scattergories*, and nonverbal communication games such as charades or *Pictionary*. The goal is to promote conversation and back-and-forth interaction.

Finally, it's important to find games that are fun for the kids. Otherwise, students with ASDs will lose their motivation, and peers will lose interest in participating.

Level of Staff Support

As we discussed in Chapter 3, the level of staff support should be carefully adjusted – enough to ensure success without providing any unneeded prompts. In group interventions, staff members must structure the time period, facilitate any games, activities, and conversations, and monitor the student with ASDs. Again, keep in mind that the group intervention is not the place for teaching new skills. Prompts should be limited to encouraging the student to participate in conversations and use the social skills that he has already learned.

Key Considerations

When designing or running a group-based intervention, it's important to stay focused on the goal: providing opportunities to practice, and thereby generalize, social skills. Group-based interventions can provide fun, bring together a diverse group of peers, or expose the students to new games or materials. These are all desirable outcomes and good by-products of these programs. However, the most important objective that will have the strongest long-term impact is the *generalization of social skills*.

One particular Lunch Bunch was impressive in many ways. A large, diverse group of peers was participating. The activities were enriching, including reading poems from Kenya, studying the dress practices of several indigenous cultures, and listening to a range of world music. A teacher and two aides were in the room. Unfortunately, from the sidelines, it was clear that the pace of the conversation was too fast for the two students with special needs – the ones for whom the group was conducted. They sat quietly at one end of the table, saying little and not understanding much of what was going on. The aides were giving them regular prompts, but even with such support, their participation was minimal. *This dynamic intervention was well staffed and exciting to witness, but it was not providing an opportunity for the target students to practice social skills.*

When you organize group intervention activities, make sure that you present and conduct the group in a way that:
- ▶ minimizes the differences between typical and special needs students,
- ▶ is respectful to the special needs students, and
- ▶ prevents negative labeling or behaviors from occurring.

You also need to be vigilant, so that you can quickly spot and eliminate any stigmas or status hierarchies that may arise within the group (or with peers outside of it). The group should be perceived by participants and by others as a fun activity that is helpful to students, rather than as a place where (higher status) typical peers patronize (lower status and stigmatized) peers with special needs.

Examples of Group-Based Social Opportunities

The Lunch Bunch

Participants. This group was organized for Wes, a fourth grader with Asperger Syndrome. He has good learning skills and manages most academic work. He also has a good level of social motivation, but has difficulties with making effective social bids, engaging in conversation, and reading nonverbal communication.

When & where. The group met once a week, during lunch, in the school social worker's office (which, while small, had a table and four chairs, along with a selection of games).

Recruiting peers. Wes chose five peers to include in the Lunch Bunch, two or three of whom would attend each time. It was a group of students who liked Wes and enjoyed playing games during lunch, so this worked well.

Training peers. Peers received no training before the group. If there were difficulties with interactions during sessions, the social worker helped Wes to advocate and explain what was troubling him or why he was acting in certain ways.

Activities. Each week, the group voted to choose a game to play. The choices included board games and card games that required participants to talk to each other.

Level of adult support. The social worker prompted Wes if he did not respond to comments by peers or if his attempts to interact went awry. She also ensured that all the students were included in conversations and had an opportunity to play different roles in the games.

Results. Wes got to practice making bids to peers and engaging in conversations in a structured setting with support from the social worker.

Classroom-Based "Friendship Center"

Participants. The "friendship center" was designed for Matthew, a first grader with PDD-NOS. Matthew had limited social motivation, and when interacting with others often insisted on doing things the way he liked. Sharing, collaboration, and turn-taking were all difficult for him. The group included Matthew, four typical peers, and the speech therapist.

When & where. The intervention occurred in a first-grade general education classroom during morning center-based learning time.

Recruiting peers. All the peers in the class rotated through the group, four at a time, for a six-week time period. The peers were grouped so that each combination contained boys and girls and students with a range of social skills. (Matthew did not seem to notice that he was the only student who remained in the group.)

Training peers. There was no training of peers.

Activities. The group engaged in highly structured, shared play activities such as drawing, building with Legos, or looking at interactive picture books. Activities were designed to require interactions, sharing, and turn-taking.

Level of adult support. The facilitators gave regular cues to enforce turn-taking, sharing, and appropriate behavior.

Results. Matthew had opportunities where he had to wait his turn, let others have their way, work on shared creative projects, and yield to the preferences of others.

Weekly Activity Group

Participants. The group was organized for Sam, a 12-year-old sixth grader with Asperger Syndrome. This was Sam's first year in middle school, and he was struggling with the transition. Sam was a fairly good student but engaged in no social interactions at school, except with a cousin. He did not respond to greetings and initiated no conversation or questions with staff or students. When others spoke to him, he remained silent with an anxious look on his face. This led others to talk for him or "rescue" him in other ways, to such an extent that he was able to get through the day without speaking. Five typical peers participated in the group.

When & where. The group met weekly in the social worker's office during a shared study hall period. They also used the gym or went outdoors.

Recruiting peers. The social worker learned that a group of peers in Sam's elementary school the previous year had been very supportive of him. He mobilized these students, asking them to participate in a "peer buddies" group.

Training peers. The participants already knew Sam well. The social worker emphasized the need to ask concrete questions and to wait until Sam responded, even if there was a protracted silence.

Activities. The group played a variety of games together. The social worker left it up to the group to decide what to play. The only requirement was that Sam was involved and that, if necessary, he had a partner to help him or a prescribed role to play, such as time keeper or judge.

Level of adult support. The social worker helped with the choice of games and ensured that Sam was participating.

Results. The group gave Sam opportunities to talk and play with familiar peers with whom he was comfortable. An unexpected benefit of this group was that some of the participants who lived near Sam started riding their bikes past his house and trying to get him to play. (At first Sam ran into the house and hid when his classmates came by! However, with encouragement from his parents, Sam learned to stay outside and interact with his friends.)

The Highly Structured Lunch Group

Participants. This group was organized for a 13-year-old with autism. Larry had limited speech and social motivation. He was working on improving his greetings, asking questions, making eye contact, and social recognition skills. Two other students with special needs were included in the group. Sixteen typical peers also participated. They were divided into two teams of eight and attended alternating sessions of the group.

When & where. The group met for 45 minutes, twice a week, in the resource room during lunch period.

Recruiting peers. The typical peers were recruited by two general education teachers, the special education teacher, and the principal. Students were told that it was a social group for a diverse group of students, some with special needs.

Training peers. Peers met with the special education teacher for one session before the group began. She told the students that Larry had difficulty talking to people and coached them to ask concrete questions, speak slowly and clearly, and give him time to respond. Good topics to discuss were also presented (e.g., favorite television programs; asking what Larry had for breakfast). The teacher also explained that Larry demonstrated motor mannerisms when he became anxious or bored, and asked his peers to give him a visual cue (hands folded in front of you) when this happened.

Activities. This group followed a formal, highly organized schedule of activities. This included looking at books of photographs and discussing what they saw, playing a geography question/ answer game, and attending a holiday party with grab bag gifts. The special education teacher inserted a high level of structure to ensure that Larry had interactions with a range of participants. She would put the participants into pairs or small groups as they played the games or discussed materials.

Level of adult support. Staff monitored Larry from across the room. If he got stuck or became anxious, they would intervene with reassurance and support. Staff would also prompt Larry to return to the group if he got up and removed himself from the activity.

Results. The group was fairly labor intensive but very effective in helping Larry to generalize his social skills. Larry was not ready for extended conversation. He was working on lower-level skills such as identifying social opportunities, making social bids, greetings, and asking/answering questions. The group gave him frequent practice opportunities for these skills with a range of peers.

Summary

Group-based interventions can provide a wide range of positive social opportunities for children with ASDs. They afford a high level of structure and control, so the adult group leaders can carefully craft the situation to allow for the practice and generalization of target social skills. When running a group, it's important to carefully prevent social stigma and to ensure that the level of structure in the group allows for optimal participation by the child.

Chapter 5

Adult Interventions and Supports

- *Adults as facilitators of social skills*
  - *At school*
  - *At home and in the community*
- *Interventions and supports*
  - *Monitor level*
  - *Guide level*
  - *Intervention level*

There are many powerful things that adults can do to help a child practice and improve his social skills. For *all* children – not just those with ASDs – grown-ups facilitate social interaction on an informal basis. Parents ask their daughter if she wants to have a friend over. For example, a caring teacher encourages a shy child to talk or play with certain peers. A Scout leader may even coach troop members to include a child in their activities.

While these efforts are helpful, they usually aren't enough to enable children with ASDs to generalize their social skills. What is needed is a more systematic approach in which a child's participation in social opportunities is ensured and guided by adult actions – actions that are faded over time as the child's need decreases. Typically, the adults who play the primary roles in these efforts are parents, activity/club leaders in the community, and teachers and aides in school.

Adult interventions are easy to apply with the youngest children as adults control most of the social interactions in preschool and the early elementary grades. However, starting in the later elementary grades and proceeding through middle and high school, the peer group becomes more and more independent in determining how children interact, converse, and play. And in adolescence, much of the peer social process is geared to run *counter* to the wishes of adult authorities as a reflection of growing independence.

Consequently, the extent of adult interventions gradually wanes over the course of development. For individuals with the strongest developmental challenges, adult interventions will remain important through the high school years and into adulthood. However, over the course of development, there is less that the adults can do. On an elementary school playground, an aide can recruit peers and organize a game that integrates the child. Young children may even consider it a special treat to have a friendly adult involved in their games.

But by high school, that's no longer the case. Teenagers generally don't want adults involved in their social interactions, and social "help" from a parent or staff member can be more stigmatizing than beneficial. So, in high school, it's often better to enlist peer mentors (see Chapter 6) or adapt extracurricular activities (see Chapter 7).

Adults as Facilitators of Social Skills

In the School Setting

In school, a number of adult staff members can be called on to help with the generalization of social skills. This includes teachers, aides, specialists, and volunteers. Because an adult has to be present during the social opportunities, teachers and aides will probably be more involved, as the specialists are more frequently providing services in their offices. On the other hand, there are situations where specialists' time is, in part, designated for classroom-based services, so they can also be involved in this process.

It is preferable to have the same person provide supports on a regular basis. That way, there will be greater consistency – thus reducing confusion for the student – and it is easier to keep track of the level of support being provided as you work to fade the assistance. In many cases, however, this is not possible. The availability of personnel dictates the use of multiple staff members in various situations. This type of model can work, but it is important to ensure consistency by maintaining communication among the people working with the child and even keeping notes on the supports that are provided.

Teachers usually have instructional or supervisory responsibilities that restrict their availability to work with individual students in social situations. Sometimes the special education teacher may have enough flexibility in her schedule to provide the needed support. More typically, it falls on the instructional aides or paraprofessionals to take on this role. Indeed, in most successful interventions, it is often the aide who plays the central role.

Aides. It can be difficult to advocate for the added expense of providing an aide for a student with an ASD. But if teaching staff and specialists cannot provide the supports in social opportunities necessary to facilitate generalization, it becomes necessary to request the support of a part- or full-time aide. Even with good social skills teaching programs, the child will make limited progress without an active generalization program.

Some school districts emphasize academic objectives and overlook the importance of social development. The Individuals with Disabilities Education Act (IDEA) and Section 504 of the Rehabilitation Act of 1973 both clearly state that the goals of an appropriate public education include teaching the skills that will lead to adult independence, full participation in the community, and a positive quality of life. For individuals with ASDs, these goals cannot be reached without effective instruction and generalization of social skills.

Aides are often put into the role of helping with academic work, but they are even more valuable for facilitating generalization of social skills. It is important that they are well trained to provide the supports we will discuss in this chapter and that they are available and present when the social opportunity occurs. In some cases, aides are hired to work on the social skills, but then given a range of other duties (from photocopying to supervising groups of students) such that they are not available during the most important times.

Training of aides. Many argue against the use of aides for fear that they will foster dependency in the child. This is often the case with well-meaning, *but poorly trained* aides, who remain at the child's elbow and provide supports that the child does not need. But this is not what is being proposed here. The aide should be trained to provide only the level of support that is needed and taught how to use systematic strategies to fade all the supports she is providing to foster independence.

The importance of training aides cannot be over-emphasized. If you are applying scarce resources to hire aides, it makes sense to train them so that they are providing as much of a contribution as possible and not undermining the team's efforts by fostering dependency. Table 5-1 lists topics that should be included in the training of aides.

Table 5-1

Training of Aides
In order for them to be effective, aides/paraprofessionals should be given training in:
1. Basic characteristics of ASDs and related challenges (communication, social functioning, restricted/repetitive behaviors, sensory functioning, learning challenges)
2. The importance of (a) providing only enough support to allow the child to be successful and (b) fading prompts and supports when no longer needed
3. The specific strengths and challenges of the child(ren) they'll be working with, as well as effective ways to instruct, facilitate social interaction, and manage difficult behaviors
4. The specific duties of their role – what they should be doing and what they should not be doing
5. Problem-solving difficult situations through the use of vignettes, role-playing, or videotapes

Teachers and other team members should observe aides on a regular and systematic basis to provide feedback about how the work is going. Aides should also be provided regular opportunities (at least monthly) to discuss with senior team members their work with the child. Finally, they should be included in team meetings so that they can give input on what they see and can hear directly from the team about program adjustments.

Volunteers. Volunteers are another school-based resource to consider, although they are useful only in special circumstances.

Most volunteers are not trained or present in the school on a regular basis and, therefore, would not be able to consistently provide the types of support we are discussing here. However, in situations where an aide is not available, a talented volunteer who is receptive to training, who is in the school on a regular basis, and who has an interest in children with ASDs may work well. In these cases, it is important to (a) screen the volunteer so you are certain that she can handle the role, (b) thoroughly train her so she has the requisite skills, and (c) ensure that she is committed to playing a regular role in this effort.

In Home and Community Settings

Outside of school, parents are the primary adults in the child's life. Parents guide the social activities of all their children, typical as well as those with special needs. They set up the play dates and register children for clubs and activities. In many cases, parents act as chaperones on field trips or serve as club leaders to ensure, through their presence, that activities are adequately structured and their child is not put in situations that are too demanding or otherwise inappropriate for him. As the child develops, the parental role generally subsides, particularly as the child enters adolescence. Nevertheless, some teens continue to let their parents guide their social efforts and are comfortable with them acting as de facto social coaches right into adulthood.

Much of the work we are discussing in this chapter falls to parents. Most parents are very busy. In many cases, both parents work, or there may be only one parent in the home. Parents have to balance the time and efforts given to the child with the ASDs with the needs of siblings, their marriage, and their employment. That's not always easy.

Therefore, it can be helpful to look for other resources in the community to help with social skills practice. This includes extended-family members, neighbors, and friends. These people can provide care, support, and social opportunities, but it would be awkward to suggest they go through formal training. Nevertheless, you can and should outline the child's special needs and offer guidelines for ways to respond to him. You can advise against providing supports that increase dependency and emphasize the importance of independence as it pertains to social skills. Some parents even develop a summary or fact sheet to give out (see Table 5-2). In many cases the child is involved in creating and writing the fact sheet. It can be done from the child's perspective (see the example) or using a third-person format.

Table 5-2

Sample Child's Fact Sheet	
Name and age	My name is Marshall, and I am 10 years old.
Description of disability	I have a form of autism, which means that I have difficulty communicating with people. I tend to withdraw and avoid people, and I like to talk to myself a lot.
Things I like or am good at	I love to talk about my train layout. I know a lot about trains and can tell what kind they are.
Circumstances that are particularly challenging for me	Loud noises can make me very upset. Also, when a lot of people are talking at the same time, I have trouble understanding what is going on.
Difficult behaviors and how to respond to them	When I get upset, I put my fingers in my ears and close my eyes. Sometimes I also make funny noises. If this happens, it helps if you tell me to put on my headphones and listen to my music.
Things that are calming or relaxing	I feel good when I can watch cartoons, listen to my music, or look at train books.
What to do in case of an emergency	My mom's cell phone is 555-1234, and my dad can be reached at 555-4321.

Many parents of younger children report that while they make frequent invitations to peers for play dates, such invitations are never reciprocated. In many cases, this results from the peer's parents feeling that they cannot handle the child with an ASD. They may not understand ASD and may be anxious about how to respond to the behavioral challenges that could occur. In such situations, offering a little informal training, providing a fact sheet, explaining about the needs of the child, and reassuring them that you will be only a phone call away, can often open the door to more invitations. (Furthermore, it serves the goal of educating the public about ASD. It raises awareness and creates allies in the effort to increase positive relations and inclusion.)

Other great resources are the club leaders, coaches, music teachers, and activity facilitators found in the community. Whether we agree with this trend or not, in today's culture, there is a heavy emphasis on organized activities for youth. From sports teams to karate, to Scouts, to music lessons – children's afternoons and weekends can be heavily scheduled times. While it is important to avoid overprogramming the child, clubs and activities can provide great social opportunities with varying levels of structure in the form of time limits, clear expectations, and concrete activities. Adapting clubs and activities to provide generalization opportunities will be further discussed in Chapter 7.

Interventions and Supports

Adults can create social opportunities in a range of settings, directly provide supports, and even orchestrate peer games and conversations. Adult intervention is one of the most powerful ways to ensure a child practices his social skills in a variety of settings. However, it carries the highest risk of prompt dependency and is the most difficult intervention to fade out. In Chapter 2, we discussed three levels of adult support and intervention (see Table 5-3). Briefly, in Monitor Level, the least intrusive, the adult's role is simply to watch interactions from a distance in order to be able to step in if the child is isolating himself, being teased/bullied, engaging in conflicts that cannot be resolved, or presenting alienating or challenging behaviors. In Guide Level, the adult serves as a coach in the situation, interacting only with the child and providing prompts, guidance, and support.

The most intrusive supports are provided in Intervention Level, where the adult provides direct support to the child but also directly interacts with the peers, recruiting participants, organizing a game or conversation, and even controlling interactions as they occur.

Table 5-3

Three Levels of Adult Support: Role Responsibilities		
Monitor Level	**Guide Level**	**Intervention Level**
Watch the child from a distance – far enough away not to have an impact on interactions, but close enough to step in when there are problems	Stay close enough to the child that you can provide information or prompts	Stay close to the child and direct his behavior so that he engages in peer interactions or games
Respond when there is teasing, irresolvable conflict, or disruptive behaviors	When the child needs it, provide information about what is going to happen, explanations about what people are communicating, and suggestions for how the child should react	Recruit peers and set up a game or activity in which the child and the peers can all participate
When responding, provide only the amount of structure and guidance needed to allow the child to recover and for positive interactions to continue	Provide needed prompts to orient to the audience, to listen, to avoid interruptions, repetitive questions/ statements, or alienating behaviors	Provide needed information and prompts as in Guide Level

The goal is to provide the lowest level of support and to gradually move from higher to lower levels as the child is better able to manage a social situation.

Monitor Level supports should be used in *any* situation where the child is not participating in social opportunities that he could manage, or where there's a potential for problems (e.g., teasing, conflict). Guide and Intervention Level supports should be applied only in the most frequent, important, and challenging situations. This usually means recess and lunch in elementary school. In middle and high school, where it is more difficult to use adult interventions, these supports can be effective in study hall, lunch, specials (e.g., gym, art, music), in the halls between classes, during extracurricular activities, and before/after school.

In general terms, Monitor Level interventions can be applied through all the grades, whereas Guide Level interventions are more easily applied in elementary and middle school, and Intervention Level is only feasible in elementary school.

Begin by assessing the situation and the child's ability to manage it. Review the 10 indicators of how difficult a situation will be for the child (see Chapter 2) to gauge how challenging it will be and what supports will be needed. As discussed in Chapter 2, consider ways to adjust the difficulty level by (a) setting up the situation, (b) teaching the situation, and (c) providing tools.

▶ Ask yourself what the peer group is doing and what they are getting out of the social opportunity. For example, when looking at a recess period, are the children blowing off steam, engaging in rambunctious play with a lot of changing groups and kids mixing with different peers? Or are there some tight and unchanging groupings, with some students sitting and talking, some playing soccer, and some playing Four Square? In the hallway between classes, are students standing around in closed groups and sharing social information (gossip) or are they engaging in fleeting interactions as they proceed to their next period? We want to coach and guide the student with an ASD to fit into the flow and function of the social opportunity, so we want to know as much as possible what that is.

▶ Consider aspects of the "hidden curriculum," the unwritten social rules and expectations that the peers are following. This includes where people are standing/sitting, the boundaries around groups, voice volume, the extent to which people are physically interacting (e.g., hugging, wrestling), and the emotional tone (e.g., excited, rowdy, serious, angry).

▶ Look in the social situation for naturally occurring groups or students who would be responsive to the child. If possible, have the child make a social bid to an already existing social group instead of having to create one.

Now let's take a more in-depth look at the processes involved at each level of adult intervention.

Monitor Level

The primary duty for the adult is to assess the situation on an ongoing basis and determine when it is necessary to step in and remove the child from the situation. To reiterate the goals stated in Chapter 1, we want to ensure that the child is engaging in successful social interactions (i.e., satisfying for all participants), that he is practicing social skills, and that he is having fun.

Table 5-4 presents a checklist of key criteria to watch for. They can be applied in many different ways, depending on the needs of the child. For some, the only concern may be aggression or severe behavior. For others, the risk of alienating peers or being targeted by a bully may be paramount. The team and the adult doing the monitoring should be clear on what the criteria are for stepping in.

Table 5-4

Monitor Level: What to Look For	
Degree of proximity to peers	☐ Is the child joining groups and remaining near his peers, or is he avoiding them?
Frequency of interactions	☐ Is he isolating himself or withdrawing into solitary play?

Degree of interaction in play activities	☐ How engaged is he with the other children?
	  ○ Playing beside them, but not with them?
	  ○ Sharing toys?
	  ○ Actually interacting?
	  ○ Participating in games or pretend play?

Communication	☐ What is the extent of verbal and nonverbal communication?
	  ○ Is he initiating and responding to greetings?
	  ○ Making basic requests and responses?
	  ○ Engaging in social conversation?

Alienating behaviors	☐ Is he engaging in behaviors that could get him teased or drive others away, such as:
	  ○ Motor mannerisms?
	  ○ Poor manners/hygiene (e.g., picking at nose or skin)?
	  ○ Repetitive questions?
	  ○ Interruptions?
	  ○ Perseverative focus on his own topics of interest?
	  ○ Shouting or using inappropriate tone of voice?

Indications of distress	☐ Is he showing indications that he is distressed and having trouble in the situation, such as:
	  ○ Talking louder or faster than usual?
	  ○ Increasing motor mannerisms?
	  ○ Withdrawing?
	  ○ Acting agitated or irritable?

Overwhelming demands	☐ Are there indications that the communication, social, or environmental demands in the situation are too difficult for him?
Disruptive/ aggressive behavior	☐ Is he demonstrating any precursors to aggressive or disruptive behavior (rumbling signs) or actually acting out?
Predators	☐ Are there students in the situation who are likely to tease, bully, manipulate, or disrespect the student?
Enjoyment	☐ How much fun is he having? Is it just hard work for him or can he relax and enjoy?

As you decide which criteria to apply before stepping in to provide support, keep in mind the overall goals for the adult-provided supervision (see Table 5-5). These goals may run counter to each other, and in many situations you have to seek a balance among them. For example, with a new student, the team may need to make the second goal (preventing problems) the priority until they get to know him. In contrast, with an older student who has been making a lot of progress and needs to function with greater independence, the third goal, fading the supports, may be most important.

Table 5-5

Three Goals for Adult Intervention
1. **Optimize successful social interactions and opportunities to practice skills.** When things are going well, the adult should stand back and let it be.
2. **Prevent significant problems,** including challenging behaviors (e.g., aggression, tantrums), alienation of peers, and teasing/bullying. It is preferable to err on the side of preventing significant problems rather than taking a chance and having to pick up the pieces later.
3. **Minimize the extent of adult interventions.** As with all adult interventions, the less the better. Always look for ways to reduce the adult role and increase the student's independence.

Some students are receptive to the observing adult taking a more active role and will let the aide provide coaching or feedback. In these cases, the following strategies are often useful.

Meeting before the situation. Before the student enters the situation, the adult can help teach the situation, give pointers, provide encouragement, set informal goals for the student to reach, and review Social Stories™ or rules/scripts.

Debriefing after the situation. It is helpful to review what went well, what caused problems, and what the student liked or didn't like.

Providing covert cues. With some students, you can devise a cue such as touching your ear or using a special word to alert them about a particular alienating behavior or concerns that they are becoming agitated. This way, the adult can provide brief feedback without ever entering the social context.

Alex

Student. *Alex was a sixth grader with a nonverbal learning disability. He was a good student and had strong social motivation. His tendency to speak at great length without giving people a chance to respond, as well as his difficulties respecting personal space, frequently alienated peers. He was also vulnerable to teasing, as he was frequently alone and easily became visibly upset when picked on.*

Situation. *In the morning when the students first arrived at the school, they'd congregate in the gym until the start of homeroom. Because of varying bus schedules, this unstructured and highly social period could last up to 30 minutes.*

Socialization objectives. *The goal of the team was for Alex to practice appropriate conversational turn-taking and to respect personal space. In this unstructured social setting, there were concerns that he would be targeted for teasing.*

Adult interventions. *Alex's aide was present during this time. She would stand at some distance and observe him unobtrusively. She arranged with Alex to give him visual cues (touching her face) when she could see that he was talking for too long or getting too close to people. She also stepped in and intervened whenever teasing would occur.*

Prompt-fading strategies. *Initially, Alex frequently looked at the aide to see if she was giving him any cues. Over time, the aide positioned herself farther and farther from Alex. As the team taught Alex more effective ways to handle the teasing, the aide cut back her support to four and then three days per week.*

Robert

Student. *Robert was a junior in high school with high-functioning autism. When young, he presented relatively high levels of challenge related to his autism, but with the support of his program he had made great progress. He was included in the general classroom for most of his classes and regularly interacted with peers at school. He had even participated in social activities outside of the school day. His conversation skills were limited, and he frequently demonstrated motor mannerisms (arm movements, hopping).*

Situation. *Robert was fairly independent during lunch. He was able to go through the hot lunch line and find a table with peers he knew from the resource room. At times, the noise and activity level of this large and poorly organized cafeteria would overwhelm him, and he'd start rocking, make unusual noises, and withdraw from social interaction. This was upsetting to the peers who witnessed it and led to several incidents of teasing.*

Socialization objectives. *The goal of the team was to have Robert engage in appropriate social interactions during lunch within this challenging environment.*

Adult interventions. *Robert's aide observed him from across the cafeteria. She could identify when he was becoming overwhelmed and would step in and escort him to a quieter room to finish his lunch.*

Prompt-fading strategies. *Initially, the aide sat at the table with Robert and later was able to stand nearby.*

Guide Level

At the Guide Level, the adult's role moves from just monitoring the child in social situations to coaching him through them. Students with some social motivation and willingness to engage with others can benefit from a guide who helps them navigate unstructured social contexts, allowing successful interaction and conversation.

In this role, the adult must carefully assess what the child needs and then provide only the guidance that is necessary for successful social interaction. The adult should take a position beside or behind the child and encourage the child to lead as much as possible. At Guide Level, the adult coaches and gives brief tips and prompts to the child, but lets the child perform the social bids, interactions, conversations, etc.

Table 5-6 presents a checklist of potential areas for Guide Level intervention.

Table 5-6

Guide Level Interventions: Areas for Coaching	
Connecting with peers	☐ Identifying appropriate peers/peer groups/ activities to approach ☐ Initiating and responding to greetings ☐ Asking other children to play ☐ Joining a group of peers in a conversation or activity
Conversation/ interaction	☐ Initiating comments ☐ Choosing topics of conversation ☐ Curbing interruptions ☐ Listening effectively ☐ Assessing audience interest in what you are saying/ not going on for too long ☐ Changing topics ☐ Managing conflict with peers
Participating in games	☐ Taking turns in games ☐ Following game rules ☐ Performing a role in a team game
Behavior	☐ Avoiding alienating behaviors (e.g., violating personal space, motor mannerisms; picking at skin or nose) ☐ Preventing behaviors that hurt people's feelings ☐ Responding to teasing

The key for the adult is to provide the most useful information without overwhelming the child or taking all the fun out of the social opportunity. Adults should *only* provide guidance when the child is struggling or losing the connection with the peers. *Too much help reduces the practice and learning and increases dependence.*

Appropriate situations to provide guidance include:
- ▶ The child is wandering without approaching any peers.
- ▶ The child is interrupting and perseverating on topics of interest, to the extent that the peers are clearly disinterested and/or turning away.
- ▶ A motor mannerism or other behavior is making the peers anxious.

Situations where intervention is *not* needed include:

▶ The child is not sharing much and is struggling to keep up with a conversation, but is attentive and enjoying the interaction.

▶ There are minor motor mannerisms that do not seem to be noticed by the peers.

▶ The child is struggling to keep up in a game, but is following the general rules and routines and enjoying himself.

At times, the adult may be targeting key behavior for intervention and, therefore, may be more quick to intervene. For example, Gordy was an 8-year-old with ASD who had difficulty respecting personal space and got too close to people, making them uncomfortable. This was a focus of his program, so the aide gave him feedback whenever behavior difficulty was seen.

At Guide Level, it is essential to build a positive relationship between the child and the adult who is providing the guidance. *The value of the guidance is directly related to the degree to which the child listens and uses it.* When the child feels that the adult is being too restrictive or critical, he will turn off, become resistant and oppositional, or demonstrate disruptive behaviors. If that happens, everyone needs to take a step back, review the way the support is being provided, and try to repair the relationship.

Even though you've moved beyond Monitor Level, you can still provide some of the student's support through covert cues and meetings before and after key situations. Always look for ways to pull back and provide less support when appropriate.

To evaluate the supports the child is receiving, ask yourself two questions:

1. Is the child engaging in successful, enjoyable interactions?
2. Are you gradually reducing the level of support?

If the answer to the first question is no, you need to reconsider the level and type of support you are giving. If the answer to the second question is no, you are fueling dependence.

Susan

Student. *Susan was a fourth grader with high-functioning autism. She had very strong visual learning skills but struggled with verbal tasks. Her social motivation was inconsistent, and much of the time she preferred to play with dinosaur figures. With prompting, she could engage in some interactions with peers.*

Situation. *At recess, Susan usually preferred solitary play or walking/marching around the edge of the playground. With support, she could sustain engagement with peer activities, but it was difficult for her. The peers in her class were very accepting of her and frequently initiated with her.*

Socialization objectives. *The goal was to have Susan spend more time in peer activities, playing games, interacting, and even having conversations. She was learning better conversation skills in her social skills group, and this was reflected in her role-playing during group. However, little social communication was noted outside of the group context.*

Adult interventions. *Susan's aide accompanied her during half of her recess time. The aide stood close to her and gave prompts. She encouraged Susan to approach responsive peers and to make social bids. She reminded her of the greeting phrases she had learned* *in her social skills group. The aide also provided verbal cues when Susan's attention was diverted from interactions or when Susan interrupted.*

Prompt-fading strategies. *The team anticipated moving to having the aide give encouragement and guidance about approaching peers, but then having Susan make the social bid by herself.*

Juan

Student. *Juan was an eighth grader with PDD-NOS. He received a high level of academic, behavioral, and social services in school. He struggled with angry outbursts that were triggered by changes in the schedule or difficult demands. He exhibited few interactions with peers or staff. In his social skills group, he was able to interact and engage in some basic conversation.*

Situation. *Juan had never been able to manage eating in the cafeteria. He usually become overstimulated and engaged in motor mannerisms or aggressive outbursts. Previously, the team had arranged for him to eat by himself in the guidance office, but they wanted to find a way to allow him to manage the cafeteria.*

Socialization objectives. *The team wanted Juan to practice self-regulation in the stimulating environment of the cafeteria and to be able to comfortably function in this setting. Eventually, they also wanted him to be able to demonstrate conversation skills in the cafeteria.*

Adult interventions. *Starting with twice a week, and building to five days a week, Juan went to lunch in the* *cafeteria, accompanied by his aide, Mrs. Brown. She shadowed him closely, monitoring his mood and ability to self-regulate. The aide verbally guided him in the cafeteria, telling him what table to sit at and where to get napkins and drinks. While they sat and ate, the aide used a self-monitoring scale to help Juan focus on self-regulation (e.g., Buron & Curtis, 2003). If Juan's behaviors started to escalate, she'd cue him to put his head down and do deep breathing. When he was clearly upset, the aide would escort him to the guidance office.*

Prompt-fading strategies. *As Juan become more comfortable in the cafeteria, Mrs. Brown was able to cut back on the frequency of the prompts. Eventually, they were able to sit with other students from Juan's classes, with Mrs. Brown facilitating conversation among group members.*

Intervention Level

For some children with higher levels of challenge, it is not enough to just monitor or even to provide a guide. These children need Intervention Level support, where the adult structures the social situation and actively directs the child and the peers in what they do. *This high level of support is for children who would not otherwise engage with peers and who have minimal skills in making social bids, interacting, and engaging in conversation.*

The goal here is for the adult to take a naturally occurring social opportunity (that is unstructured or presents demands beyond the child's ability to process) and insert enough structure so that the child can participate. So, instead of wandering the periphery of a disorganized playground, he can interact and play games with peers. Or, rather than sitting quietly by himself at lunch, he can engage in some conversation with peers while eating.

At Intervention Level, the adult needs to size up the social context and then create a structured situation within it that will allow for the child to participate. In some cases, the adult can use naturally occurring groups of peers or games that are already going on. However, having an adult directly involved in an activity usually fundamentally changes its nature, so you may lose participants. In most cases, carefully choose peers and enlist them to join a game or conversation of the adult's design.

When choosing what type of activity to engage in, it is helpful to review the criteria of difficulty from Chapter 2. Briefly, the child's level of social functioning will determine the number of peers to include, the length of time, and the type of demands to build in.

Selection of peers. The first step is to identify and recruit the correct number of peers. The rule of thumb is that the greater the degree of challenge for the child, the fewer participants to include. Invite peers who like the child and who are good communicators with patience and strong social skills.

Choice of activity. This will depend on the child's level of skills. You want something that the child can manage without too much difficulty. Any good turn-taking or interactive game will work, but find games that are attractive to the child and the peers. If they do not want to play, it will be harder to keep the interaction going.

If the child cannot handle conversation or verbal intercourse, passing a ball or playing a form of tag will work. For situations where you want to emphasize practicing conversation and communication skills, you can use verbal games or structured conversations. For example, a number of games require players to come up with an alphabetical list of objects ("I visited my grandmother and I packed an alligator ... banana ... cabbage ... dump truck ...," etc.), or play "telephone," where children pass a whispered message from one group member to the next as they sit in a circle to see how the message gets mis-heard and changed. Have a couple of choices ready, in case one activity does not capture the group's interest.

"Structured conversations" are conversations where you ask the group a concrete question of interest and then give each participant a chance to answer it. Good questions include "What is your favorite flavor of ice cream?" and other food preferences. (Some children with ASDs who have dietary challenges may become uncomfortable with this, but for most it provides great modeling for eating a range of foods.) Other good questions address favorite television shows, favorite colors, and things the children did over the weekend.

It should be a question that is easy to answer and calls on the individual to express an opinion or preference, or share an experience. The adult takes a very active role, directing who should speak and when. Establish a pattern of everyone taking turns and having to participate. A good variant to try is to have everyone ask questions of the person who just answered the previous question.

It's important to establish a boundary around the game or conversation. For example, if children are constantly joining and leaving the group, it becomes confusing and can overwhelm the child with an ASD. Moving the group to an unoccupied corner of the room or playground is the easiest way to set the boundary. If this is not possible, it may be necessary to direct children who are not participating in the activity to engage with other peers.

During the activity, provide enough prompting and coaching for the child to participate, at least minimally. This may include giving cues for the child to:
- ▶ Initiate a greeting, small talk, or conversation

- ▶ Respond to comments or questions from others
- ▶ Reduce interruptions
- ▶ Stay on topic
- ▶ Make eye contact and use nonverbal communication integrated with his words
- ▶ Take his turn at the appropriate time

The adult may also help by giving conversation starters or topics, explaining what is being communicated by others, helping the child to read nonverbal gestures, and giving coaching on how to best play the game.

At Intervention Level, the amount of support may be fairly high. However, as with at the Monitor and Guide Levels, it is important to only give support that is needed and to always look to reduce support when it is not needed. As soon as you can, pull back from verbal prompts and coaching and start using tools such as conversation starters, rule cards, or scripts. Provide less structure in the game or conversation as the child is more able to function on his own. Ultimately, you want to move through Guide Level and Monitor Level and eliminate the adult intervention altogether.

Paul

Student. *Paul was a third grader with PDD-NOS. He was verbal, but had echolalia and did a lot of perseverative scripting (repeating long monologues from favorite TV shows and movies). He frequently retreated into solitary fantasy play about his favorite cartoon character, Marmaduke. Paul required a high level of structure to follow the classroom routines, but with intensive one-to-one instruction was able to learn and had made regular progress. He demonstrated minimal social motivation and little attachment to the peers in his class.*

Situation. *If left alone during recess, Paul only engaged in solitary self-stimulatory play or fantasy play about Marmaduke. He enjoyed going outside and sometimes resisted coming back in at the end of recess.*

Socialization objectives. *The goal was to give Paul experience with basic peer interactions through structured turn-taking games and to provide opportunities for communication with peers.*

Adult interventions. *Paul was given 10 minutes of "Marmaduke Time" at the end of recess if he engaged in peer play for the first part of recess. His aide shadowed him, providing prompts and guidance and steering him toward social opportunities. The aide also recruited appropriate peers and organized games of tag, passing a ball, or relay races. The choice of games gradually evolved toward word games and indoor board games that required more communication. During the games, the aide actively facilitated the interactions, ensuring that Paul was fully participating.*

Prompt-fading strategies. *Over time, the amount of "Marmaduke Time" was reduced. As Paul mastered the routine of the games and interactions, the aide reduced the frequency of her interventions. Eventually, Paul was coached before recess to ask certain questions of the peers when given a visual cue from the aide.*

Anna

Student. Anna was a second grader with high-functioning autism. She had a split program, with half of her time spent in the general classroom and the other half in the resource room. She was a good learner and was keeping up with most grade-level academic objectives (with modifications), but she had great verbal challenges. She initiated little speech and struggled with voice volume and articulation. She was liked by her peers, who would regularly approach her, help her with her work, or play with her at recess. However, she had poor interaction skills and could only provide a limited response to these overtures.

Situation. During lunch, Anna's classmates from the general education classroom sat at the same table in the cafeteria. This was an extremely social time with children talking and laughing.

Socialization objectives. The team wanted to take advantage of the lunchtime social opportunities by facilitating peer interactions for Anna. She needed practice with basic conversation skills: listening, making eye contact, asking questions, taking turns.

Adult interventions. Anna's aide accompanied her to lunch. The aide recruited peers to sit at a separate table with Anna in the cafeteria. Starting with just two peers, the group grew to include up to four. The aide facilitated the conversation, asking questions of the children and prompting Anna to respond when she needed it. The aide expected Anna to respond to all questions or comments that were directed to her and to ask at least one question during each lunch period. At the end of the period, the aide gave each participant a sticker.

Prompt-fading strategies. *Over the course of the year, the aide reduced the frequency of her prompts. As Anna was able to manage it, the aide gave her assignments before lunch (e.g., ask one question, make good eye contact) and wrote them on a card for her. In the spring, the aide moved the group back to the class's assigned table.*

Supporting Staff and Monitoring Progress

At all three levels of intervention, deciding what supports to use, how far to go, and what is "just right" versus "too much," are all difficult decisions to make. However, most well-trained aides and other school staff have the skill set from working with children to read a situation and intervene effectively. The challenge is to stick to the basic principles:

- ▶ Provide *enough* support so the student can *be successful* in social opportunities while applying the skills he's learning
- ▶ Provide *no* supports the child *doesn't* need
- ▶ Look for ways to provide less support over time through *fading* the interventions

One way to enhance the performance of aides and other staff providing direct support to the child is to give them an opportunity to discuss how interventions are working. This may be done through individual meetings with the special education teacher or one of the pupil personnel staff, or it can be discussed at team meetings. In addition to supporting the aide, the team should also be systematically monitoring progress to ensure that (a) the interventions are effective, (b) supports are being faded as soon as possible, and (c) the program is being changed when necessary (see Chapter 3). A form like the one in Table 5-7 is easy to use and provides a systematic approach to tracking the child's progress.

Table 5-7

Assessment Form for Adult Interventions			
Student _____	Date _____		
Situation _____	Adult Providing Support _____		
Target Skills	Using Without Prompts	Using With Prompts	Not Using
	☐	☐	☐
	☐	☐	☐
	☐	☐	☐
	☐	☐	☐
Supports Being Provided			
_____			
_____			
_____			

Summary

Adults can play a key role in facilitating social opportunities. This includes parents, school team members, and community-based activity leaders. Adult interventions are among the most powerful at adapting a situation to fit a child. However, they are more difficult to implement with middle and high school students, and they are usually the most difficult supports to fade.

We classify adult interventions according to how intrusive and directive they are. Monitor Level adult supervision just includes watching the child and heading off trouble. At the Guide Level, the adult provides coaching and some prompts to support the child's social functioning. Intervention Level includes the most intrusive actions by the adult, such as recruiting peers, organizing a game or activity, and providing prompts to the child. No matter which level of intervention the child needs initially, the goal should always be to fade supports as quickly as possible.

Chapter 6

Peer Mentors

- *The advantages and disadvantages of peer mentors*
- *Setting up a peer mentoring program*
- *Mobilizing groups of students as peer mentors*

"**P**eer mentors" are typical schoolmates, friends, or other peers who provide support to the student with an ASD in a naturally occurring social activity (e.g., Bellini, 2006; Dunn, 2006). That can mean sitting at lunch, attending a school dance, walking between classes, going on a Scout camping trip, or any other social situation that presents challenges for the child with ASDs. The duties of a mentor vary depending on the demands of the situation and the needs of the student. *The goal is to provide the supports in the most naturally occurring way possible.*

Advantages and Disadvantages of Peer Mentors

There are several advantages to using peer mentors when you're trying to help a student practice and generalize his social skills.

First, peer mentoring is a very flexible type of intervention that can be adapted to a wide range of situations. A peer mentor may give prompts, help draw the student into conversations with his classmates, or just act as a familiar, supportive person to whom the student can look for guidance or reassurance. Moreover, a peer mentor can provide support in many settings where an adult would draw undue attention to the child. For example, having a grownup sit at the lunch table with a student or accompany him at a dance would put a significant damper on the social interactions that occur. A peer mentor, on the other hand, draws far less attention, and allows the student to practice his social skills in a more natural setting. It also means that the student gets needed support without having to add duties to the team members or hire new staff.

Second, peer mentors are a free, naturally occurring resource. They're already in the social setting that you want to help the child access. And most groups of teens and "tweens" offer support to one another. Just look at how they'll respond to peers who have encountered illness or loss, or who are struggling with the ups and downs of dating, cliques, and school pressures. In most groups, there are usually one or two kids who become known as the good listeners or the informal "therapists" for their friends. Those are the peers you want to recruit. Then you can formalize the relationship by providing some training, setting clear role expectations (i.e., what to do, when, where), and perhaps offering service time credit, course credit, or other informal recognition.

With peer mentors, students get more than just helpers who support them. They also get the opportunity to learn additional social skills through modeling (i.e., learning by watching and imitating others). In social situations, the individual with special needs gets a close-up look at how it is done and how a range of social challenges are handled. For many students with ASDs, imitation and modeling is difficult, but to the degree that it can occur, peer mentoring provides an ideal opportunity, as they are in actual social situations watching others interact.

Best of all, in some situations the peer mentorship relationship develops into a true friendship. Affection, shared enjoyment, respect, humor, and common memories are the building blocks of any friendship. As they occur between a student and a mentor, the relationship sometimes grows beyond the mentorship and enriches both the mentor and the student with special needs. And even if a true friendship does not develop, the relationship between the two students fundamentally changes the attitude of the mentor toward students with disabilities and gives the individual an ally or peer resource within the school environment.

It's somewhat ironic that in peer mentorships, the mentors usually get as much – if not more – out of the program as the child with special needs does. When mentors receive appropriate training, support, and recognition, they usually derive great enjoyment, satisfaction, and learning from their role.

Table 6-1

Benefits of Being a Mentor
1. Mentors learn about autism and develop a new set of communication and support skills. With good training, mentors can successfully navigate the interactions and are not left frustrated or confused, but rather with a sense of mastery and connection to the individual with the ASD.
2. Mentors are directly helping a student who might otherwise be isolated from the peer group and vulnerable to teasing or bullying. The good feeling that comes from helping another person can often lead a mentor to get beyond the usual petty concerns of day-to-day social life, competition, and peer pressure.
3. When the relationship goes well, it also allows the mentor to really get to know the student with autism. It can bring mentors to understand how the student experiences the world from a different perspective, and to appreciate the engaging quality of individuals on the spectrum that is shared by parents and professionals who work with this group.

Despite the many benefits of this type of intervention, there are some challenges. Peer mentoring requires careful planning and consideration of several issues in order for it to work well. For example, it is essential to recruit the right peers, provide appropriate training, and set up the intervention so that it will fit within the specific school environment. Also, there is less control in this type of support. As opposed to a group-based intervention where you can regulate many of the conditions, with peer mentorship you often have to plan as much as you can and then adjust factors as they arise. The issue of social stigma – of people looking down at the child with autism because they have a disability – is also more of a challenge with peer mentorships. You must design, present, and execute these programs in a respectful way, providing help and support while affirming the individual and de-emphasizing the disability.

Setting up a Peer Mentorship

There are five vital steps involved in setting up an effective peer mentorship:

1. Identifying the situation, event, or setting where you want to provide support
2. Designing the role of the peer mentor
3. Recruiting the peer mentors
4. Training the peer mentors
5. Monitoring the program as it is rolled out through observation from a distance and debriefing the participants

Let's take a look at each of these steps in detail.

Step 1: Identifying the Situation

Peer mentors potentially can be used in almost any situation. Generally, give priority to two types of events – those that are key social times during the day and those that are causing particular challenges for the student.

Of course, kids interact all day long in school, but their busiest social times tend to be first thing in the morning (getting settled/homeroom/morning work time), lunch, recess, study hall, specials (gym, art, music, etc.), and after school as they're leaving.

Socializing also occurs with increased intensity during transitions. For the older students, that means passing between classes. For elementary school students, transition periods occur between learning activities (e.g., when they've finished math and are getting ready for social studies). Other key social times include extracurricular activities and special events such as field trips or assemblies.

Outside of school, key social situations may include play dates, Scouts, sports, or after-school recreation clubs (e.g., Boys and Girls Club, YMCA). If the student is not socially participating during one of these social occasions, you may want to consider using a peer mentor.

When deciding how to use peer mentors, it is also important to consider situations that are particularly challenging for the student. You can identify these events because they lead to teasing/conflict with peers or distress for the child. For example, if the student routinely gets teased in the hallways or when he is at his locker, a "hallway buddy" intervention may be helpful.

In one case, Robin was frequently getting set up by peers to act inappropriately at the local tennis club. Her parents recruited a peer mentor and soon these difficulties ended.

Step 2: Designing the Role of the Peer Mentor

This is one of the most difficult steps in peer mentoring. In general terms, the mentor is there (as a peer) to provide guidance and support in order to allow the student to take advantage of social opportunities and prevent withdrawal, conflicts, or behavioral problems. The specific duties of the mentor are slightly different in each case and need to be clearly defined (and explained to the mentor) and monitored to ensure appropriate follow-through.

It is essential to design the mentor's role to be respectful to the child with special needs. One of the most common reasons why a child with social skills challenges resists peer mentoring is that he feels that having a mentor will make him stand out as being "different" or deficient in some way. This is especially true for the highest functioning students with ASDs. It can be very painful for *any* child to feel like he doesn't fit in. He may fear that the presence of a peer mentor will label him as "retarded," "stupid," or "damaged goods." That's why, throughout the process, you must convey the message that the mentor is there to help with the *typical* challenges that the student struggles with, *not* because he "has a problem," is autistic, is immature, or "doesn't think the same as others."

Sometimes, the mentors themselves may try to approach their role too aggressively. Everyone needs to understand that the mentor is, first and foremost, the student's peer. She is not a parent, an authority figure, a baby sitter, or a teacher. When a peer mentor takes too dominant a role, it is unfair to both the student with ASDs and to the mentor. It is disrespectful and undermining to the student's identity as a member of the peer group. Furthermore, it puts too much responsibility on the mentor.

In one case, a well-meaning middle school mentor took on a very maternal and punitive stance, at times doing too much (e.g., carrying the student's books) and at other times being openly critical and bossy. Needless to say, this did nothing to assist the student's social functioning. It is usually helpful to think of the mentor relationship as two *partners* working together, rather than a supervisor and a subordinate.

Design the mentor role around the demands of the situation, the needs of the student, and the natural skills of the peer. Take, for example, a student who had difficulty finding his seat each day in a large, noisy cafeteria. The team recruited a peer mentor to meet the student outside the lunchroom and walk in with him. In another case, the team recruited a peer who was particularly good at conversation and humor, and then carved out time in the school day for the two to engage on a-one-to-one basis.

Make sure to gear the mentor's role to the age of the child. Most students under 10 cannot provide much beyond being a designated partner for an activity and following one or two directions. It is only in middle school and beyond that mentors are able to guide, orient, and facilitate social interactions. (Some precociously mature mentors are exceptions to this. However, in these situations, it still is important to avoid putting too much responsibility on the mentor.)

Table 6-2 presents a list of duties commonly assigned to peer mentors, as well as a list of duties that should *not* be performed by mentors.

Table 6-2

Duties of a Peer Mentor	
Commonly Assigned Peer Mentor Duties	**Duties That Should *Not* Be Performed by Peer Mentors**
1. Physical guidance/orientation	1. Setting limits or enforcing rules
2. Asking questions and making comments to involve the student in conversations	2. Criticizing or giving overt negative feedback (constructive feedback is acceptable)
3. Introducing the student to peers	3. Giving orders to the student
4. Cueing the student to perform certain appropriate social behaviors and to stop performing inappropriate social behaviors	4. Talking to teachers or peers for the student
5. Including the student in games or activities	5. Teaching other peers how to respond to the student
6. Explaining comments, jokes, or confusing interactions	6. Providing unneeded supports

Step 3: Recruiting the Peer Mentors

It is essential to find the right peers to act as mentors. The right classmate or teammate will be one who demonstrates good social skills, enjoys being with the student in question, has a good relationships with other peers, is reliable, and has good social problem-solving skills (see Table 6-3).

Table 6-3

Desirable and Undesirable Qualities of Peer Mentors	
Desirable	**Undesirable**
1. Friendly	1. Vulnerable to peer pressure
2. Good social and communication skills	2. Heavily involved in clique or exclusive peer group
3. Strong connection to a peer network	3. Quiet or reserved
4. Empathetic, able to look at situations from more than one perspective	4. Sarcastic or biting sense of humor
5. Comfortable interacting with peers from different social groups	5. Poor communication skills
6. Good sense of humor, but doesn't need to be funny all the time	6. Unusual, disruptive, or negative behaviors
7. Follows through with commitments	7. Frequently late to commitments – or doesn't show up at all
8. Punctual	8. Negative attitude towards people with disabilities or other minority groups

It can seem daunting to enlist peers into social activities with children with special needs. It requires finding the right group of peers, structuring the activity in the right way, and building in rewards. In elementary school, most students are compliant with adult expectations and readily participate when asked. However, in middle and high school, students form cliques and become more limited in the range of peer contacts and activities they allow. Further, different schools and towns have distinct peer cultures that define how students regard each other, interact among themselves, resolve conflicts, and support the school. Some peer cultures are highly competitive and exclusive. Others are more supportive and accepting. In some very challenging environments, peer cultures can be violent and destructive.

In most schools, there are groups defined along the following parameters: popularity ("cool kids"), athletic participation ("jocks"), academic achievement ("brains"), social awkwardness or shyness ("nerds/geeks"), shared interest in certain activities (e.g., "skaters," "motorheads," actors/musicians), and involvement in drugs or other illegal activities. The labels change from school to school, and some groups are more dominant in certain peer cultures.

When you're trying to decide who would be good participants to recruit, the popular kids might look like a logical choice. They have strong social skills and are usually developmentally a little ahead of their peers. However, this group is usually very exclusive and tends to alienate others who don't measure up to their standards. These students are also usually very active in maintaining their position in the group, and therefore are less motivated to take time away from their friends. Many of the other cliques are also problematic as their interests are restrictive, they engage in teasing and put-downs, or they have limited social skills of their own.

In most schools, the students who make the best peer mentors are the ones in groups oriented toward academic achievement or musical/dramatic performance. They frequently are the teachers and human service workers of tomorrow. They are accepting, have an understanding of diversity, and enjoy helping others. This is the group that you want to find and mobilize. They readily participate in the activities and, even more, enjoy them and provide student leadership to your efforts.

It can be effective to start your search with social networks that are closest to the student. Look at students in his classes or with whom he spends significant time during the day. In some cases, there may be connections from the neighborhood or from community-based clubs. Family relationships can also be helpful. For example, a cousin or the friend of a sibling might make an appropriate mentor. If these strategies do not yield appropriate mentors, widen your search by talking to a range of teachers and checking with service clubs, Honor Societies, or theater and music groups. Or, if there are clubs that focus on topics that interest the student (e.g., chess, computers, animé), check with faculty advisors to see if there are any candidates in those groups.

Awards/initiatives. Before recruiting peers, the team should establish what formal or informal credit will be given to the mentors. Schools often give course credit or time towards a service requirement for students acting as mentors. In many cases, no formal credit is needed. The mentors become interested and enjoy the role so much that they are willing to do it without extra compensation.

Giving formal credit has its advantages and disadvantages. It can help to emphasize the importance of the mentors showing up on time and carrying out their roles to the best of their ability. On the other hand, the credit can attract students who are more motivated to get the course credit or fulfill a service requirement than to be peer mentors and work with a student with ASDs.

In general, it is good to find ways to recognize and thank student participants. They are, after all, taking time out of their schedules and giving something back to their community. Recognition at awards ceremonies, articles in the school paper, segments on the school television show, or mention during school announcements can help to communicate how important their efforts are. Letters of recommendation and other documentation that can be used in college applications are also powerful ways to recognize a peer's contribution.

When recruiting, it is important to fully explain the role and its requirements to the peers so that they can make an informed decision about participating. As much as possible, indicate the what, where, when, and why of the mentoring. This should be done without mentioning the name of the student with the ASDs to protect confidentiality until the mentor candidate agrees to participate.

If you present the peer mentoring program in positive, interesting terms, you'll get better results. Not many students will sign up to "spend time with students with special needs." But many will want to join a new diversity initiative, help out with a human relations club, or participate in service club activities. As much as possible, frame the opportunity as an honor or privilege – one that reflects the positive status of the potential peer mentor. In other words, you are recruiting the student because of his social skills, interpersonal sensitivity, and leadership skills.

Adding frills to the package can help. Food is a great enticement. Serving pizza or providing brownies increases the interest level. Meeting in a desirable room, using high-tech equipment, and having access to special privileges can also enhance the motivation. At the same time, avoid a high-pressure sales approach. It can be hard on everyone when a student agrees to be a mentor but then finds that it is not for him and has to withdraw. Rather than pushing ambivalent students into trying mentoring, it is preferable to err on the side of having fewer, but more committed mentors.

Step 4: Training the Peer Mentors

Appropriate training is an essential component of effective peer mentoring. Without it, mentors are vulnerable to making mistakes, failing to provide needed supports, or acting in disrespectful ways toward the student.

Training is an essential component of a program's success – so be sure to schedule it *before* the mentoring begins. Your training program can be anywhere from 30 minutes to two hours or more, depending on the extent of the mentoring role that you are requesting. You can conduct the training on a 1:1 or small-group basis, but make sure to do it in such a way that the mentors can ask questions, express concerns, and give their input on how to best manage the social situation during which they will provide support.

If the student with ASD is comfortable with his diagnosis and is motivated to have a peer mentor, it may make sense to include him in the training. That can be tricky, though, because there is a danger that the situation inadvertently becomes disrespectful, with people speaking as if the student is not in the room or referring to the diagnosis in a way that objectifies the student or his challenges.

In most cases, if the student is not present at the training, you'll want to explain to him that the peers are being given some basic information about him and instructed on how to be a mentor. In some cases, teams have tried to conceal the occurrence of the training from the student. In general, avoid "secrets," because when they're revealed (and they usually are at some point), it severely undermines the student's trust.

Topics to include. Start out peer mentor training with the message that everyone is good at some things and not so good at others. Point out that the student has a range of talents or relative strengths, but struggles with communication and social functioning. *Avoid* using clinical or diagnostic terminology. That type of language can get in the way of mentors experiencing the individual as a "real" peer or someone that they can get to know. It places the emphasis on the autism rather than the person.

The following are topics that you should be sure to cover in any peer mentor training.

The role of the mentor. When you explain the duties you'd like the mentor to perform, be specific, but keep it simple. Describe the key things you'd like him to do, such as stay/sit/walk with the student, talk with him, introduce him to other kids, ask him questions, play games with him, and/or give him cues in response to certain behaviors. Be sure to include *when* and *where* the mentor should show up and *how long* his responsibilities will last.

How to respond to specific behaviors. Be as specific as you can about the behaviors that the student may present, describing them in easy-to-understand and non-inflammatory terms. For example, you can say he may "move his arms in a flapping motion," "stare at his hands," "make noises that sound like a machine," or "walk on his toes." You want the mentor to know what to expect, not to be upset by it, and to feel comfortable with it. If there are behaviors you want the mentor to ignore, let him know that. If there are specific behaviors that hamper the student's communication or social interactions, teach the mentor appropriate ways to respond to them. For example:

▶ "If John withdraws, looks down, or walks away, ask him a question about the last class he was in."
▶ "When he starts to hop or rock, make eye contact (gently touching his shoulder if necessary), and say 'Quiet body.'"

- "If he repeatedly interrupts or changes the topic without a transition, ask him to wait a minute until you are finished talking about the topic at hand."

Proactive problem-solving. Try to anticipate likely occurrences or things that could go wrong, and talk the mentor through ways of dealing with them. Examples include:
- the mentor being held up and unable to be there on time
- schedule changes due to weather-related delays
- fire drills
- unfamiliar peers joining in the interactions or games
- unexpected teasing/bullying
- peers engaging in misbehavior
- staff questioning what is going on

While it's impossible to cover every contingency, the more planning and discussion that goes on beforehand, the better the chance that you can prevent difficult situations.

Questions and comments from the mentor. Be sure to give the mentor plenty of opportunities to ask questions about his role and what he should expect. It's also helpful to ask for the mentor's input about the situations you are addressing. As a student, the mentor will likely know more about some of the peer group's unwritten rules and range of acceptable behaviors than you do. Take advantage of his expertise to best understand the situation at hand.

Step 5: Monitoring the Program

Once you've got the peer mentoring program underway, ongoing monitoring will help to keep it on track and to avoid problems. Initially, staff should observe the situation from a distance and be ready to intervene when needed. Once you know that the mentors are providing the needed supports and the situations are working, observation may no longer be necessary. However, you should still schedule periodic check-ins with the student with ASD, meetings with mentors, and spot observations.

In this process, focus not just on anticipating and preventing problems, but also on tracking growth in social skills, and identifying opportunities to reduce the level of support provided by the peer mentor. Also assess the participation of the mentors on an ongoing basis to see if further training is needed, if they are losing motivation or "burning out," or if more mentors should be recruited to lessen the load.

Mobilizing Groups of Students as Peer Mentors

Up to this point, we have been discussing using individual students as peer mentors in designated situations. There are also ways to mobilize groups of students to provide less structured supports to a child with ASDs (e.g., Schlieder, 2007). The peer group is a powerful resource. Naturally occurring groups can be enlisted in efforts that can create more opportunities for social interaction in the natural setting for students with ASDs. The "Circle of Friends" model is an example of this type of strategy, which has been around for some time and is now being effectively applied to children with autism (see Schlieder, 2007).

Many creative school staff members have effectively used this type of strategy. For example, Mel was a high school student with Asperger Syndrome who had difficulty initiating and responding to greetings in distracting settings such as busy hallways or the cafeteria. Mel's guidance counselor, who was also a faculty sponsor of one of the service clubs, enlisted the members of the club to greet Mel when they saw him and to give him time to come up with a response to their greetings. This provided valuable practice opportunities in the natural setting and allowed Mel to build his greeting skills.

Another more general intervention occurred at a middle school where Honor Society students started a lunch invitation program. Participants in this program would look for students in the cafeteria who were eating alone and ask them to join them for lunch. The program was not limited to students with ASDs, but available to any student who was eating alone. Students could choose to turn down the invitation, but regardless, it was a powerful statement of inclusion, addressing the isolation of many students.

Yet another great example of this strategy is a middle school where the seventh and eighth graders were recruited to be playground mentors for the fifth-grade recess.

Will

Will is a fifth grader with an ASD. One day at recess he decided he wanted to play baseball and picked up a whiffle bat and ball. At first, Will wandered around the playground by himself. He approached his aide several times and asked her to pitch to him. She appropriately encouraged him to find some peers to play ball with. He wandered some more and then crossed paths with a girl who was a playground mentor. She tried to engage him in conversation and then asked him to play ball. He accepted her invitation and, as she was pitching to him, several other fifth graders approached and joined in the game. When it was time for Will to give another student a turn, the playground mentor talked to him about the importance of taking turns, and Will relinquished the bat. He later took a turn pitching. Without any staff involvement, Will went from wandering the playground on his own to playing ball with the other kids, talking to them, and even joking around with them.

The greatest challenge with this type of intervention is creative thinking. You need to identify naturally occurring groups of students who would respond to a call to reach out or support others and then come up with a way for them to be helpful. Typically, you would provide some general training to participants, but not as rigorous as what you'd do with individual peer mentors. If the program is to target an individual or small group of students with ASDs, it is important to discuss it with them, get their approval, and let them know very clearly what will happen and when.

If you present and carry out this type of intervention in an effective manner, the experience can be very empowering for the student. (Of course, if it is poorly organized, is inconsistently done, or results in stigmatizing or disrespectful approaches to the student, it can undermine social motivation and backfire.)

Disability Education Interventions

One strategy used to mobilize groups of students aims at teaching them about the disability of one of their classmates. This approach is frequently used when an elementary school student has cancer or a neuromuscular illness. However, in recent years, disability education programs have been used very effectively for individuals with ASDs (e.g., Wagner, 1999).

These programs arose out of situations where aspects of a child's illness or disability confused peers or made them uncomfortable or anxious, consequently leading to social isolation, rejection, or even scapegoating of the child. The risk of these outcomes is particularly high when the illness or disability leads to changes in appearance, the presence of wheelchairs or other equipment, frequent absences, or unusual behavior.

The objective is to have the child, or his parent or doctor, teach the class about the illness or disability in age-appropriate terms. A typical program might include explaining about the child's appearance, behavior, or equipment; telling them how to be helpful to the child; and answering questions. This type of intervention typically reduces the peers' anxiety, increases their social connection with the child, and even mobilizes them to become helpers to the child. When applied to youngsters with ASDs, the focus is usually on explaining any unusual or disruptive behaviors, suggesting ways to engage the child in conversation or play, and emphasizing how important it is to include the child in social activities.

Disability education interventions are usually performed in elementary school for several reasons. First, the elementary classroom forms a clearly defined social group and environment where the child spends most of the day. So it is a natural group to educate. Once students start changing classes every period, it's harder to find a time and place where you could reach everyone the child encounters during the day. Second, during the preadolescent years, teasing and scapegoating among peers increases, making the risk of stigma and negative fallout greater. However, with proper planning, there are occasions in middle and high school where this type of program can be effective.

It usually isn't necessary to consider a disability education intervention before the third grade. Younger children have a limited ability to understand the objectives of the education and are usually still accepting of a wide range of children.

A disability education program can create powerful positive changes at school. However, sometimes parents, teachers, and the child himself are uncomfortable with ASDs being discussed so directly. This anxiety is well founded, as there is a potential for this type of program to lead to stigma or disrespectful treatment at the hands of peers. It is important to follow these guidelines:

- Plan the disability education intervention carefully. Under no circumstances should it be approached casually or be performed with little lead time. Consider the school's policies with regard to sharing this type of information and ensure that you have administrative support. Sometimes, school policy will dictate how it has to be delivered.
- Start with discussions with the parents. If they want to consider it, offer the idea to the child. Give the child as much control as possible over how it is carried out (e.g., when, where, by whom). Do not proceed if the child does not approve of the idea.
- Decide if the child will be present during the training. This should be left up to the child. If he is not comfortable being present, he should not attend. In some cases, the child welcomes the opportunity to tell people about ASDs, and this should be encouraged.
- Consider what level of clinical terms to use. In some cases, labels such as autism and Asperger Syndrome are shared with the audience and explained in terms they can understand. In other cases, more broad and less pathological descriptors are used such as a "condition where it is difficult to talk and understand people, play with friends, and control your behavior." Clinical labels should only be used if the child is completely comfortable with them and uses them himself.[1]
- When choosing who will do the presenting, include people who can describe the challenges and make recommendations to the peer group *in terms they can understand*. This

---

[1] While some individuals with ASDs are comfortable with discussing their diagnosis using clinical terms, others strongly resist any mention of it. Usually, children with Asperger Syndrome or more challenging forms of autism are comfortable with the diagnostic terminology as it helps them to better understand their behavior and the world. In contrast, individuals with PDD-NOS have enough social perspective-taking to see the impact of a clinical label and the possible stigma involved. They resist anything that makes them "different" from the peer group. This factor should be carefully assessed through discussion with the child before attempting a disability education intervention.

might be the parent, a teacher or school-based specialist, or a community-based therapist. In some cases, the child himself can present. This has the advantage of putting him in control and in the role of an expert.

▶ Be careful when selecting the audience. Include only peers who know the child and see or interact with him regularly in school. Other students will just get confused by the discussion and lose interest. Also, take care to exclude any peers who might be inclined to use the information to tease or scapegoat the child. *If this cannot be done, do not proceed with the intervention.*

▶ Carefully prepare the content and coordinate presentations, if there will be multiple speakers. Use a diversity approach, pointing out that everybody is good at some things and not so good at other things, and then presenting the strengths and challenges of the child. Include:

- A description of the child's strengths and challenges, in terms that the audience can associate with the behaviors they observe on a daily basis. Include information about the student's interests, pets, favorite television shows, etc. – information that is not related to ASDs. This helps the peers view the child as a "regular" student, just like them

- Key challenges that have impact on the peers (e.g., problems with understanding what people say, difficulties paying attention, tantrums or aggressive behavior)

- Strategies for the peers (e.g., talk slowly and clearly, play certain types of games)

- How peers should handle commonly encountered difficult situations

- An opportunity for questions and discussion

▶ Throughout the process, be careful to treat the child with respect, as a full member of the peer group. It is helpful to think of the student as a *person* with a disability – an individual who is much more than just his disability. Guard against infantilization, disrespect, labeling, or defining the child just in terms of the autism.

Peer Mentors in Action

Ken

Student. *Ken was an eighth grader with Asperger Syndrome. He was very bright and did well with his studies. He was extremely verbal with family members, but avoided interactions with staff and peers at school. When people approached him, an anxious look would come over his face, which made people tend to "rescue" him and do the talking for him. Consequently, he demonstrated few if any interaction skills. His difficulties also reflected significant challenges with perspective-taking, understanding emotions, and nonverbal communication.*

Social situation. *The team wanted to use the lunch period to give Ken an opportunity to practice interaction skills with peers outside of his family.*

Role of the mentor. *The team recruited Barry, who was in several of Ken's classes, to be a peer mentor. Barry's role was to accompany Ken to lunch two days a week and to have Ken sit with him and his friends. Barry was to make efforts to include Ken in the conversation by introducing him to friends, asking him questions, and pausing at times to give Ken a chance to enter the conversation. Barry was given training before he started and met with Ken's special education teacher on a monthly basis to update her on how it was going.*

Outcomes. *At first, Ken sat at the table in the lunchroom and said nothing. With time, he began to answer some questions and to make comments to others. By the end of the school year, Ken was comfortable enough in the group to initiate conversations about his favorite interest (video games).*

Barry's mentoring role evolved as well. Now, instead of just trying to help Ken join the conversation, Barry learned to give Ken cues when he needed to take a breath and give others a chance to speak!

Rebecca

Student. *Rebecca was a sophomore in high school with PDD-NOS. She was in a mixed program with most of her instruction occurring in the resource room. She attended specials, social studies, and science in the mainstream. She was comfortable with the peers in her special education classes, but not with those in the mainstream. She could sustain conversation with some peers and even developed several friendships that carried over outside of school.*

Social situation. *Rebecca had never gone to a dance and wanted very much to attend the fall dance at the high school. Her parents were concerned that she wouldn't be able to handle it, but the school team felt that, with the right supports, Rebecca could be successful.*

Role of the mentor. *Rebecca had a cousin, Mary Beth, who was a junior at her school. She volunteered to serve as a peer mentor for Rebecca at the dance. Mary Beth worked with Rebecca's parents to shop with Re-*

becca for a dress, practice dancing, and coach her on how to behave. Her special education teacher took her to the gym on the day of the dance, so she could see ahead of time how the lights and decorations looked and how the music would sound.

Rebecca's parents drove Rebecca, Mary Beth, and Mary Beth's boyfriend to the dance. At the dance, Mary Beth stayed with Rebecca except when she danced with her boyfriend. Mary Beth also arranged for a boy to ask Rebecca to dance. After Rebecca had been at the dance for 90 minutes, her parents checked with her via cell phone. At that point, she decided that she was tired and was ready to go home.

Outcomes. *Rebecca had a great time at the dance and was able to practice getting dressed up, mixing with peers, and even dancing. She went to the next dance, again with Mary Beth, but this time she spent most of the evening with peers from her classes.*

Michael

Student. *Michael was a seventh grader with PDD-NOS. Michael had good expressive and receptive communication skills, but struggled with perspective-taking, managing transitions, sensory processing, nonverbal communication, and following the hidden curriculum. He had two good friends who attended a different school. In his own school, he was fairly isolated. He often made highly provocative statements that tended to alienate peers. The school was a regional middle school program that served a wide range of students, some of whom had conduct disorders.*

Social situation. *Michael experienced great difficulties in the crowded hallways between classes. He had difficulty when being bumped or when he accidentally brushed up against other students. His locker was next to that of a student with strong antisocial tendencies who, seeing Michael's isolation and atypical features, began to target him. He called Michael "gay" and "loser." This student's friends would often congregate around his locker and gang up on Michael. Michael responded by arguing and returning insulting comments, which only aroused more teasing.*

Role of the mentor. *The team felt that it was important to protect Michael from this bullying treatment. Disciplinary actions against the other student had been only marginally successful. So, the team tried recruiting a "hallway buddy" for Michael. Looking through a list of peers who were in most of Michael's classes, they found Don and Joey, who both agreed to participate. They arranged schedules so that one of the two was always with Michael as he transitioned between classes. They set it up so that it was minimally disruptive to the mentors, yet provided a presence for Michael. The mentors were told about Michael's disability and given training about their roles. They were to walk with Michael, talk to him, and wait by his locker while he exchanged books and got what he needed. If there was any trouble, they were to inform the teacher and administrator. Initially, the vice principal was stationed in the hallway nearby during the change of classes, but this was found to be unnecessary.*

Outcomes. *The "hallway buddy" system worked extremely well. The presence of a peer stopped the teasing. Not only was Michael not alone, but there was an* *eyewitness to any misbehavior that went on. Michael developed stronger relationships with Don and Joey and began talking to them regularly.*

Ian

Student. *Ian was a 9-year-old third grader with PDD-NOS. He had cognitive abilities in the average range, but learning disabilities related to writing and math made academics challenging. Ian's behavior had an immature quality. His speech was at a kindergarten level, and his choice of play activities was similarly delayed. In general, the peer group in the classroom ignored him. At recess Ian stayed by himself. At times he would watch his classmates playing, but he'd retreat from any opportunities to join in. Once in a while, he'd play make-believe games with a child from one of the first-grade classes.*

Social situation. *Staff wanted to help Ian engage with his peer group so that he could practice his social skills, particularly age-appropriate communication and play. They targeted recess as a great opportunity.*

Role of the mentor. *The team recruited Nicky to be a peer mentor at recess two days per week. Nicky's job was to hang out with Ian for most of recess and to help him to join in games. Nicky was told to give Ian encouragement and help teach him about the games. If Ian refused to follow him, Nicky was to let him go. The team emphasized to Ian that it was important to play with his classmates, and explained to him that Nicky would be helping him join in.*

Outcomes. *With Nicky's support, Ian was able to successfully join in the playground games on most days. Other peers who saw Nicky being a peer mentor asked if they could try it, too. Two other boys were subsequently recruited and served as playground mentors on other days. Nicky's participation in the games gradually grew. Eventually, he reached the point where he enjoyed playing with the other students and talking to them. In fact, he made several lasting friendships as a result of the intervention.*

Summary

When it comes to creating social opportunities for children with ASDs, peer mentors are invaluable. They are naturally occurring resources, able to provide support in situations where adults would be unwelcome. In addition, they can be positive role models – and potentially friends – for the student with social challenges.

A peer mentorship program requires careful planning, but the outcome can be significant. In fact, the peer mentors typically get as much out the program as the child with autism.

Individual mentors, though, aren't the only way to get peers involved in helping a child with ASD practice and improve his social skills. Some programs mobilize a *group* of peers to reach out to students with special needs. Others provide educational programs that help children to better understand and interact with their classmates with ASDs.

Chapter 7

Adapting Extracurricular Activities

- *Assessing activities*
- *Supports and accommodations to consider*

Extracurricular activities – in school or in the community – can provide good social opportunities for children and teens with ASDs. They're generally more structured than other social activities. Time limits, planned and scheduled activities, clear expectations, and the presence of an adult leader are all elements that can make a club or team more predictable and, therefore, less challenging than more impromptu or informal get-togethers.

Of course, how appropriate or socially challenging a given extra-curricular activity is depends largely on the adult leader. Some have direct or indirect experience with ASDs and know how to effectively communicate and interact with the child. Others may not have the skills, but are willing to learn and are committed to including the child in the club/activity. Unfortunately, there are also many leaders who are uncomfortable, anxious, or rejecting of children on the spectrum. Many use a rigid approach and are not willing to make changes for a child with special needs.

For example, in sports, some coaches take a highly competitive approach and would not welcome a child who not only could not immediately contribute to victories on the field, but who needed extra help and a flexible approach. Other coaches emphasize participation, sportsmanship, and fun over the win/loss record. Their teams are more able to provide social experiences that will allow the child to practice and expand his social skills.

Finding the Right Fit

Recently, at a meeting of parents of adolescents with ASDs, two dads were discussing their sons' experiences in Scouting. One boy was in a small troop with a very supportive Scoutmaster. He enjoyed the meetings and camping activities, made friends in the troop, and had progressed to the level that he was seeking his Eagle badge. The other teen was in a larger troop that took a more rigid approach to meetings and trips. He felt alienated and was frequently teased by the other Scouts. Not surprisingly, he quit the troop after a year.

There are several important lessons in the scenario presented above. First, it is important that parents carefully interview youth leaders to see if their approach fits the child. Second, it is helpful to "keep knocking on doors" until you find a club/leader who is a good fit. Even though you may find a number of inappropriate teams, troops, and clubs, the good ones are out there – and if you keep looking, you may find them.

It's usually unrealistic to expect adults in the community to attend classes or read lengthy books about ASDs. But parents can develop a short summary description of their child's challenges, effective ways to respond to challenging behaviors, and strategies that might work to allow greater social participation (see the Sample Child's Fact Sheet in Chapter 5). In situations where you feel comfortable that the adult will respect confidentiality, this can be in the form of a fact sheet on ASDs with specific examples/applications to the child.

Whenever possible, observe the activity – as discreetly as possible – to see how things are going. Also check in frequently with the adults working with the child (at least monthly). Give them a chance to bring up any difficult situations and to ask questions. Addressing little problems and making them go away is much easier than waiting until they become big problems. Once the group leader is calling you on the phone to say that it isn't working and that the child can no longer participate in the club/activity, it may be too late to salvage the situation.

As always, it is important to monitor how the child is doing. Looking back at our original objectives from Chapter 1:
▶ Is the child engaging in successful social interactions?
▶ Is he practicing social skills?
▶ Is he having fun?
▶ Is he overly stressed by participation?

When things are not working well with an activity or club, parents often ask how long they should persist before they give up and move on to something else. Usually, you'll want to decide up-front an initial trial period to ensure that the child has an opportunity to get comfortable and give the activity a real chance. That could be as little as three meetings or as long as a school semester, depending on the commitment expected by the club or team.

How soon will you be able to tell whether the activity is actually helping the child expand his social skills? That can vary. In some cases, observable benefits are evident very quickly. In others, they can come on slowly and subtly, not becoming apparent until the child has been participating for 6 to 12 months. Usually, the best measure of whether to stop going comes from the child's behavior. If he appears upset or stressed before meetings, or if he resists going, carefully re-evaluate whether to continue. Before deciding to pull the child out, though, make sure to get feedback from the leader. Often, a child may put up some resistance, but have a good time and participate well once he's there. The reason for stopping should not be that he needs more time to play video games, but that the activity is too demanding or does not provide appropriate social opportunities. And, of course, any recurrent teasing or scapegoating of the child would be a clear indication to stop attending.

Assessing Activities

Before enrolling the child in a given activity, it's important to assess whether it is appropriate and whether it can provide social opportunities. There are several factors to consider.

Time and Schedule

There are three questions to ask with regard to time and schedule.
1. How long do meetings/practices last? Shorter time periods are usually preferable, at least at the beginning, as fatigue and sensory issues can overwhelm the child if the activity goes on for too long.
2. What time of day does the activity occur? If meetings are after school and this is a time when the child is usually recovering from the challenges of the school day, it may be difficult to make it work. For another child, night or early morning meetings might be difficult.

3. How many practices or meetings are scheduled on a weekly basis? In middle and high school, some teams or clubs practice every day after school. That could be overwhelming for many students, because they'd get no afternoons off to recover or rest.

Type of Adult Facilitation/Leadership

The ideal adult leader is both *highly organized* and *flexible*. He presents a well-structured meeting or practice with high levels of predictability, routine, and clear expectations. Yet, he is comfortable with adapting the rules and routines for individuals with special needs. Some leaders take a hands-off, "laid-back" approach with few rules or procedures. That may work for many clubs and students, but for children with ASDs, it can lead to difficulties understanding the environment and knowing what to do. Other leaders take a very rigid approach to extracurricular activities. They run their groups in a very structured manner, with clearly stated demands and rules, but without any room for modification. You often see this on competitive sports teams. This type of environment is generally a bad idea for students with ASDs, as they may not be able to fully comply with the rules or demands, which can lead to criticism and negative attention.

It's also important to look for adult leaders who are warm, perceptive, and tuned in to the social patterns in the group. Some experience with autism, in their work or personal lives, is a great asset. The leader's style of communication is another extremely important factor. Adults who speak quickly and use a lot of complex language, jargon, or figurative expressions will make everything more challenging for the student.

You want to find leaders who are equally accepting of all participants, not just the best performers. In many clubs or teams, a status hierarchy develops, with the more skilled or popular students getting more attention, praise, and coaching. That's not conducive to success for students with ASDs or other special needs, and they will be at risk to become marginalized.

Demands of the Activity

Among the most important considerations are the demands that a given activity places on the child. If the demands are too great or don't fit the student's profile of strengths and challenges, you are potentially putting him in a situation that could be chronically aversive and frustrating. That's not to say that you can't try clubs, teams, or activities for which the child does not have well-developed skills. Most participants in children's activities are beginners, and the point of the club is to build skills while having fun.

However, there are some types of activities that we know children with ASDs typically find more frustrating and difficult to learn. This varies across individuals, but in general, team sports with ball play require quick information processing and decision-making relative to the flow of the game, and that is often very difficult for individuals on the spectrum. In contrast, track, swimming, and martial arts are all sports that do not have these types of demands. In addition, they have a higher level of repetition and routine in practice, which fits well with the learning and coping style of children with autism.

Similarly, with regard to musical instruments, percussion, piano, or brass instruments with fewer valves are often a better fit than strings or woodwinds with a large number of controls, which require integration of listening, finger placement, and/or movement of the bow. (Of course, some individuals with autism *do* have talents in, say, soccer or violin. If that's the case for a particular child, it could be a good course to pursue.) Conversely, some individuals on the spectrum have little or no performance anxiety and are good at memorizing scripts. If that's true for a child, drama activities could be a great fit.

A second set of demands surrounds the ambition level of the club, team, or activity. Highly selective, competitive, or well-known groups (e.g., sports teams, musical groups) often require members to attend lengthy practices, care for elaborate equipment, and travel to performances or games. If the child has a special talent, consider having him participate in a group that will allow him to develop it further – and give him the opportunity to interact with other students with similar talents and interests – but carefully weigh all the demands to ensure that they are not overwhelming.

Child's Interest in the Club Activities

A primary consideration when choosing an extracurricular activity is the child's interest in the club. A high level of interest brings built-in motivation to participate and manage challenges. A lack of interest can lead to boredom and will add to the level of difficulty for the individual. Clubs devoted to science, video games, animé, or technology are often good avenues to pursue for students with ASDs.

Peers Who Participate in the Club

When looking at extracurricular activities as social opportunities, it is essential to consider who participates in the group. Are there peers who will be outgoing, inviting, responsive, and even open to becoming friends? Does the club attract students who are supportive to students with disabilities? Or are there members who are given to teasing and bullying?

The size of the club or group should also be considered. It's harder for a child with an ASD to make social bids and carry on successful interactions in a big group.

Types of Social Interactions That Occur

Depending on the activity, the style of the leader, and the routines, clubs present varying levels of opportunities for peer interactions. For example, let's look at the bands at two local high schools. In the Jefferson High band, the director gives his group frequent breaks, during which the students sit and chat with the peers sitting next to them. There's also a lot of socializing during the warm-up, and students tend to hang around after practice and talk. In contrast, the director of the Lincoln High band is highly focused and forbids any conversation during rehearsals. Students sit quietly, listening to the director and waiting for a cue to start playing.

For obvious reasons, the Jefferson High group (although a less accomplished band) provides a much better social opportunity. In some clubs and teams, there is a more social climate and participants frequently interact while practicing or working on activities. In others, this is not the case. Observing a meeting/practice or checking with some of the participants can often provide valuable information in this regard.

Sensory and Other Environmental Factors

Sensory challenges can also affect whether an activity will be a good fit. This varies from individual to individual and sometimes is difficult to predict. However, reviewing the student's sensory challenges ahead of time may help you to head off some problems.

Dan

Dan, who has Asperger syndrome, was invited to be a statistician for his high school's basketball team. Every-

thing went fine during practices. But once the real games started, Dan found that the sound of the scoreboard buzzer was extremely jarring for him, even painful. Despite trying various strategies (e.g., ear plugs, desensitization), after a while it became clear that the distress caused by the buzzer could not be overcome, and the challenges of the activity outweighed the social opportunities.

When thinking about whether an extracurricular activity is appropriate for the child, it can be helpful to consider how much the club/activity requires:

▶ going outside or in the water
▶ being exposed to unusual or loud noises (e.g., machine noises, alarms)
▶ touching or manipulating textures (e.g., modeling clay, building materials)
▶ being exposed to odors (e.g., food, horse barns)
▶ using equipment or wearing uniforms or head gear
▶ preparing and eating food

There are many strategies for addressing sensory challenges. So, if a great opportunity arises, even if it involves sensory experiences that you think will be difficult for the child, it may be worthwhile to try adaptations. For example, you might be able to block the sensory input (using, say, ear plugs or sunglasses), modify the clothing/equipment, implement desensitization procedures, or adjust the sensory supports (e.g., deep pressure, jumping, chewing) that the child already uses in other settings. In addition, if he's really interested in the club/activity in question, the child's motivation to participate may help him to confront and overcome the sensory challenges, thus providing further benefits.

Don't forget to consider other environmental factors beyond those that impact sensory functioning. For example, Roger was very uncomfortable in rooms with high ceilings. He needed to wear a hat with a brim to keep him from looking up. Other students have fears of the water or certain animals. Those fears could affect their participation in outdoor clubs or 4-H.

Availability/Possibility of Providing Supports

In most situations, it will be necessary to provide supports of some type (which will later be faded) to ensure success. This is easier to do in some clubs/activities than in others. For example, it is easier to adapt the workout in an individual sport such as track or swimming than in a team sport where participants conduct drills as a group. Or, it is easier to modify the degree of physical support and type of instruction in a martial arts class than in rock climbing, where you are tethered to a wall or rock face. (That's not meant to discourage rock climbing. There are some successful climbing programs for individuals with special needs.)

Again, the possibility of adding supports depends in large part on how flexible the leader is and how competitive the group is. There are high school drama clubs that include students with ASDs in leading roles. They provide extra coaching, give line prompts when the student becomes nervous, and adapt make-up and costumes. Other programs systematically exclude these students because of the "artistic standards" of the director or group.

You may come across opportunities where it is difficult to provide supports, but the benefits of participation make it worth the extra advocacy and effort. However, in many situations, it makes sense to find another club or team that is receptive and encouraging when adapting the program for an individual.

Table 7-1 presents some of the advantages and disadvantages of common types of extracurricular activities.

Table 7-1

Potential Advantages and Disadvantages of Common Extracurricular Activities		
Activity	**Potential Advantages**	**Potential Disadvantages**
Sports: Team	• High social status • Many opportunities for peer interactions • High level of routine in practices	• Fast processing speed required for ball play • High-pressure, ambitious approach • Competitive and often socially unsupportive athletic culture
Sports: Individual	• Many opportunities for peer interactions • Repetition/routine in training • Judged on performance, not social skills • Clear indices of improvement • Opportunity to compete against oneself	• Focus on winning that can lead to frustration and poor self-esteem
Martial Arts	• Repetition and routine in training • Emphasis on relaxation and discipline • Emphasis on ethics, morality	• Emphasis on aggression and violence that can lead to misconduct • Exotic, spiritual aspects that could be confusing • Rigid approach by some instructors
Music	• Participation with pro-social peer group • Repetition in practice • Opportunity to practice on one's own • Appreciation from the audience • Range of instruments to choose from, depending on skill set	• Anxiety related to performance • Ambitious or high-pressure approach • Daunting processing challenges

Activity	Potential Advantages	Potential Disadvantages
Table 7-1 (continued)		
Drama	• Participation with pro-social peer group • Emphasis on rote memorization • Multiple jobs available: performing, building sets, running the lights, selling tickets	• Anxiety related to performance • Ambitious and high-pressure approach in some programs • Actors required to express emotion • Limited number of performing roles (i.e., potential for rejection)
Debate Club/ Model United Nations	• Participation with pro-social peer group with many opportunities to interact with peers • Exposure to useful information related to political affairs and social policy	• High demand for verbal skills • Sometimes highly competitive and contentious atmosphere • Anxiety related to performance • Complex topics being discussed
Scouts	• Highly social activities with a pro-social group of peers • Concrete recognition of accomplishments through badges and ranks • Exposure to camping, nature, and survival skills • Explicit pro-social set of guidelines to follow	• Sensory challenges related to nature and camping • Many situations that require independent functioning • Troop approach may be more or less inclusive
Interest Clubs	• More motivation to participate • Access to peer group with similar interests • Opportunity to share interests with others	• Social interaction not necessarily built into activities

Table 7-1 (continued)		
Activity	Potential Advantages	Potential Disadvantages
Horseback Riding	• Contact with a peer group at the stables • Sense of mastery and control fostered • Attachment to the horses	• Sensory issues (especially odors) • Peer interaction not necessarily required
Fishing/ Hunting/Bird Watching	• Popular activities that can provide connection to a peer group • Potential wealth of interesting information and skills	• Not inherently social activities; can lead to more solitary approach
Religious Youth Groups	• Contact with pro-social peer group • Explicit pro-social message, encouraging fellowship	• Exclusionary message or high-pressure approach in some groups • Intolerant attitude towards disability in some groups

Supports and Adaptations to Consider

Once you've identified a club or activity that you think might be appropriate for the child with an ASD, the next step is to find the right combination of supports or adaptations to ensure a good social opportunity. You can usually use the interventions discussed in Chapter 3 – teaching the situation, tools, incentives/ reinforcers – to alter the social difficulty of most extracurricular activities. (It may take some tweaking before you get the supports to the right level, so it's a good rule to expect the student to commit to three to five meetings or practices before deciding whether to continue.)

Here are some more adaptations and supports that are often used to make an extracurricular activity more socially accessible for a child.

Changing the Duration of Meetings/Practices

Have the child only attend for a part of the meeting at first. Start with the easiest and most enjoyable activities and then gradually build.

Changing the Frequency of Meetings/Practices

Attending only some of the meetings is another way to prevent the child from being overwhelmed or fatigued. The risk, though, is that he won't experience the same continuity as the other members, which could lead to frustration and make it more difficult for him to make friends.

Providing Rest and Snacks Beforehand

Most clubs and teams meet after school, when the child may be tired. He might be more likely to have a successful experience if you can build in a rest period during the afternoon before the activity.

Assigning the Student a Role/Job

For many teams and clubs, a separate role can be assigned to the student. The best example is on a sports team, where the student might serve as a manager. In Scout troops, the child can be provided duties and roles that are adapted to fit him (e.g., collecting firewood, taking attendance). Make sure, though, that the other club participants demonstrate appreciation and respect. If "managing" the team means chasing errant soccer balls and picking up dirty towels dropped on the locker room floor, the team members may wind up treating the child as a low-status servant rather than a peer.

Using Peer Mentors

Clubs and teams are great opportunities to use peer mentors (see Chapter 6). Having a peer support the child at meetings, activities, or practices, may allow him to participate on a much deeper level – and have more fun as well. Some local recreation departments have programs that match trained peer mentors to youngsters with special needs, in order to make activities more inclusive.

Adult Supports

Often, adult activity leaders can provide needed supports for a child. In small groups, they can see how the interactions are going and jump in whenever necessary. They can also assign partners or groups that best fit the child's needs. In general, avoid situations where two captains pick teams or peers form groups spontaneously, as the student with an ASD will likely be picked last or will not know how to join a group. If these situations arise, it is usually best for the adult leader to step in and assign the student to the group or team that will work best for him. The leader can modify the role and duties to meet the strengths of the child.

In larger groups, you'll probably need a second adult such as the assistant Scoutmaster or assistant coach to monitor and provide supports. In school situations, the child may need an aide's help to participate in extracurricular activities, even if they fall outside of the formal school day.

Recently, there was a story on the news about a young man with autism who helped out with his high school basketball team. Late in a game, there was an opportunity to let him play. He was an excellent outside shooter and, once in the game, sank five shots in a row. The fact that he made all the baskets gave the story the entertainment value that led to it being picked up by the news media. But the really impressive accomplishment was the way the coach, players, and school created this social opportunity for the young man. They gave him many opportunities to practice his social skills with coaches, teammates, and fans. All treated him with respect and were sensitive to his disability. Demands were adjusted so he could be successful. And, he was having a lot of fun.

Here are some more examples of how programs have used extra-curricular activities to help students practice their social skills.

Mark

Student. *Mark was a freshman in high school with a diagnosis of PDD-NOS. He was very quiet and became anxious when interacting with others. He received a high level of academic support, attending most of his classes in the resource room. He participated in a social skills group but had very few interactions throughout the day. He felt comfortable speaking with only one of his peers in the resource room.*

Extracurricular activity. *In order to provide more social opportunities, Mark's parents and teachers encouraged him to join the cross-country team in the fall of his freshman year. He was very reluctant, but his parents made his access to video games contingent on trying the team for at least a month.*

Socialization objectives. *The special education team hoped that daily practices and frequent meets would give Mark opportunities to spend time and interact with peers. Mark experienced significant challenges with his conversation skills, nonverbal communication, perspective-taking, and comfort with social experiences. At the least, they hoped the cross-country activities might, over time, lessen his anxiety about social events.*

Supports. *Mark received a number of supports. The coach appointed two peer mentors (one was a team captain and the other a freshman), who regularly approached Mark, conversed with him, and checked to see that he was comfortable. During team runs, one of the* *two usually ran with Mark, so he was not isolated. At first, Mark was given an adapted work-out regimen, as he was not accustomed to strenuous physical activity. Over the course of the first year, he reached a point where he could keep up with the slower runners. The coach took an interest in Mark, encouraging him and giving him some individual instruction. Before meets, the assistant coach would give Mark special briefings about the courses.*

Outcomes. *Mark wound up participating in cross-country throughout his high school years. Freshman year, he ran in the freshman meets and finished most of the races. By his senior year, he earned a varsity letter and was among the top 10 runners on the team. He regularly attended team social functions and became comfortable greeting his teammates in the hallway and making small talk with them. Over time, Mark made several friends on the team and had regular contact with them outside of school.*

Gordon

Student. *Gordon was a junior in high school with Asperger Syndrome. He was a "B" student, with good verbal abilities and an excellent memory, but he had challenges in reading comprehension, writing, and math. Gordon talked in class and interacted with a range of peers throughout his school day, but he had no real friends and didn't participate in any social activities outside of school.*

Extracurricular activity. *At the urging of his special education teacher (who was also an the advisor to the drama club), Gordon joined his high school's drama* club during his freshman year. For the first two years, he mainly helped with the lights and sound system, enjoying all the equipment in the control room. During his junior year, the advisor asked him to play a speaking role in the show. Gordon agreed and handled the role extremely well.

Socialization objectives. Gordon's team hoped that belonging to drama club would provide him opportunities to talk to other kids from school, collaborate with them on projects, attend cast parties, and, ultimately, make some friends.

Supports. When Gordon took his first speaking role, the director gave him extra coaching. Initially, he was allowed to rehearse in private. Later, he went through readings and rehearsals with the full cast. His special education teacher attended the rehearsals and provided encouragement and situational teaching throughout. Several aspects of the role were adapted to eliminate difficulties for him.

Outcomes. Gordon played his role well and received praise from people throughout the school community. This meant he had to return greetings and learn to graciously accept compliments. He attended the cast party and left early when he started feeling tired and overwhelmed. He also began to sit at lunch and talk with several drama club members he'd worked with on the show, and even started hanging out with them outside school.

Stan

Student. *Stan was a 12-year-old seventh grader with PDD-NOS. He was a thoughtful, quiet youngster who could talk at length about his favorite topics (Star Wars, game shows) but struggled with age-appropriate reciprocal conversation. He had no friends but was close to his brothers and several cousins. Stan sometimes experienced meltdowns or angry outbursts when faced with sensory challenges, unexpected transitions, or unfamiliar situations.*

Extracurricular activity. *Stan's family signed him up for Boy Scouts. His older brothers were all Scouts, so Stan's parents and the Scoutmaster were well acquainted. The Scoutmaster had met Stan at several family picnics. Prior to enrolling Stan, his parents met with the Scoutmaster and discussed Stan's needs. The Scoutmaster did not have any experience with individuals with ASDs but was motivated to learn and open to taking a flexible approach.*

Socialization objectives. *The parents hoped to give Stan opportunities to engage in social interactions with peers outside the family. They also wanted to help him become more independent and to practice coping with sensory and transition challenges.*

Supports. *Before Stan joined the troop, the Scoutmaster read some books and spoke with the parents at length. He then worked with the other troop leaders to adapt the scouting routines to Stan's needs. Stan was allowed to take breaks during troop meetings. He was given extra instruction in marching, camping skills, and badge requirements. The adult leaders made sure that* one of them was always available to respond if Stan's behavior started to escalate. The leaders even arranged for Stan to get a gradual exposure to camping. On the first camping trip, he just made a day visit. On the second, he was able to spend the night, and on subsequent trips he became comfortable spending multiple nights away from home. The Scout leaders handpicked Stan's tent mates and work partners to ensure that he received peer support.

Outcomes. Stan quickly mastered the routines of the troop and grew to enjoy camping, even though he was uncomfortable with some of the sensory aspects of it. He experienced some minor conflicts with peers but no one teased him, and he improved his communication skills over time. During his third year, he was able to befriend a younger, new member of the troop.

Amy

Student. Amy was a 9-year-old third grader with PDD-NOS. She was a very bright student but had limited communication skills and significant motor mannerisms (moving her hands near her face). Amy avoided interacting with other children, but had a special interest in horses.

Extracurricular activity. Amy's parents signed her up for riding lessons at a local stable to increase the frequency of her social activity and to give her more experience communicating and working with adults. The stable provided private lessons, periodic competitions, and an opportunity for children to help out with the work around the stable.

Socialization objectives. *Amy's parents were hoping that their daughter would have opportunities to communicate with her instructor and the group of youngsters who hung around the stable helping out.*

Supports. *In consultation with the parents, the instructor slowed down the pace of Amy's program and did not push when she appeared reluctant. Amy was given many chances to observe how things were done and to practice with spotters nearby. Amy's parents offered her incentives (money towards the purchase of toy horses) for the time she spent with the peers at the stable. They also hired one of the older members of the stable, a junior in high school, to serve as a mentor, checking in with Amy and providing guidance when needed.*

Outcomes. *It took six months for Amy to become comfortable riding. Talking to the other girls who hung out at the stable was even more challenging. But after a year of coaching and support from her mentor, Amy was able to interact independently with her peers as she worked in the barn. She developed a strong attachment to one of the horses and loved to spend time brushing and talking to it. Amy continued at the stable throughout her adolescence and developed a number of friendships. During high school, she became a youth leader at the stable and a mentor to younger children.*

Summary

School- and community-based extracurricular activities can provide excellent opportunities for a child or teen to interact with his peers and practice his social skills. These activities often have a lot of built-in structure, which makes it easier for the child with autism to cope. Of course, each club or team has its own culture, ranging from flexible and inclusive to highly competitive. That's why it's important to assess each opportunity's level of difficulty and to see whether it's a good fit for the child. In many cases, supports and accommodations can be provided that will enable the child to participate successfully.

Chapter 8

Final Thoughts

- *Reviewing the objective*
- *Initiating efforts to create social opportunities*
- *Final words*

Reviewing the Objective

Individuals with ASDs confront a range of social challenges. When putting together a plan to address a child's social skills difficulties, you need to keep in mind not just his immediate needs, but his long-term ones as well.

One goal of any program should be to make sure the child learns enough social skills so that he can function independently in the community as an adult. Even a "loner" must be able to deal with store cashiers, landlords, police officers, and others. Anyone who's going to support himself with a job needs to have the basic social skills to interact with supervisors, coworkers, and clients or customers. In short, even if an individual chooses to have no friends, a certain level of social competence is required to live independently in our society.

A second important goal is helping the child master sufficient social skills so that, as an adult, he'll be able to *choose* how much social activity he would like in his life. Never assume that, because a child seems uninterested in other kids *now*, that this will always be the case. Some individuals with ASDs are socially motivated from a young age. But many who start out having limited or no social motivation during childhood reach a point in adolescence or early adulthood when they want to have friends and be involved in social activities (e.g., Carter et al., 2005; Schopler & Mesibov, 1986). Sadly, if that time comes and they haven't developed social skills, they find themselves excluded from the peer group and unable to connect with the people around them. When that happens, the individual often is left depressed, feeling that he has missed out on an important aspect of his life. There still will be young adults with ASDs who choose to remain isolated, engaging primarily in solitary pursuits. You can't control how a child may choose to live one day – but you can help ensure that he has options to choose from.

Learning and generalizing social skills is a dynamic process. As he grows, each child is confronted with constantly changing social demands. In preschool playgroup, the other 3-year-olds will probably accept him as long as he obeys the "share" and "no hitting" rules. By high school, peers expect the highest order of communication skills, including social problem-solving, perspective-taking, and empathy. Every year there are slightly different expectations to be met if a child is to "stay in the game."

Most children's social, language, and communication skills develop at roughly the same pace as the social demands for their peer group. Their social skills develop with only temporary and limited periods of difficulty. But when a child has an ASD, his individual development doesn't keep up with the increasing social demands and he is at risk of falling further and further behind his peer group. You can combat these challenges by teaching him necessary social skills *and giving the child opportunities to practice them, so that he will generalize them and use them in the whole range of social opportunities he will encounter.*

It's difficult for children with ASDs to generalize new social skills from the teaching environment to the real world. In order to do so, they need to be involved in *a variety of regular social opportunities in which they can participate successfully, practice social skills, and derive enjoyment.* That means finding or creating social opportunities and providing the right supports so that the activity is not too difficult and the child can have fun. It also requires effectively fading these supports to build independence.

We know, based on experience, that this approach can facilitate social development in a powerful way. It can build social motivation in the individual, open doors and make connections within the peer group, and change attitudes in the peer culture. It does not take away the challenges of developmental disabilities, but it builds on the skills of the individual to allow him to more fully participate in the social world around him. It allows him to better access the benefits of a social community (e.g., support, care, enjoyment) and to function more independently as an adult in social, work, and community settings. Moreover, in many cases, it has an impact on the peer group, changing attitudes and helping to build understanding about the challenges of autism spectrum disorders.

Initiating Efforts to Create Social Opportunities

If you're starting out in a school or community setting where this type of intervention has not been tried, pulling together the necessary resources and getting the key people on board can seem daunting. But you'll find that the time and effort are worth it, as interventions get put into place and the child starts participating more and more in the social activities around him.

For any of these strategies to work, you need the buy-in of the key players involved. School principals and special education managers are ultimately responsible for what goes on in their programs and, therefore, need to understand and support the plan. Parents, of course, have a large stake in all aspects of their children's school programs. Teachers, therapists, and aides often have the most impact on a program's success. And, none of these interventions would be possible without the participation of the child's peers.

Buy-in is a tricky thing to understand and assess. Many people will go along and say that they agree with the plan (especially if their boss or a strong parent tells them to do it), but then fail to follow through or take responsibility for making things happen because they don't really understand or support the ideas being proposed. For most of us, change is hard. Once we have developed our own ways of doing ours jobs or caring for our children, we are reluctant to try new ways of operating.

Consequently, when proposing strategies to create social opportunities, you may hear:

▶ "We can't waste the typical students' time with this. They have to prepare for mastery tests, take courses for college, go to sports practice, etc."
▶ "The typical students won't give up lunch with their friends to sit with kids with special needs."
▶ "The parents of the typical students will never give us permission. They won't want their kids wasting their time with students with special needs."
▶ "I don't have the time or staff to do this."

These arguments may sound reasonable on the face of it, but they have little support in practice. In fact, experience has shown that, when these programs are well designed:

▶ The typical students get as much (if not more) out of the program as the kids with special needs. They learn about disability and life, develop more accepting attitudes, and make new friends. (And it looks great on college applications!)

▶ Many typical students enjoy participating and gladly forego other social activities to help out.

▶ Parents of the typical students support good programming and, when they understand the program, readily give permission for their children to participate. In fact, when complaints from parents arise, it is usually because their children were not included in the program.

▶ The interventions can be carried out without undue time demands on staff and often can *save* time as more of the social program is delivered by peers.

You will need to assess buy-in and, if everyone's not on board, address the issue. These interventions are fairly easy to put in place if you have the support of the team members. Without that support, however, the process becomes very difficult (although not impossible).

Final Words

For the parents, school teams, community-based professionals, and individuals with ASDs who are engaging in this process, here is some final advice.

Keep It Fun

If people aren't having a good time, or your efforts feel like hard work without much benefit, take a step back and find a way to *make* it fun. Use humor to incorporate the children's interests, and involve people who know how to have a good time. There will be situations that require hard work and perhaps cause a bit of anxiety; fun is your ally and an important tool to help deal with difficult times.

Help People Become Comfortable with Unfamiliar Strategies

In many settings, the interventions discussed in this book have not been tried and, therefore, may seem foreign, unfeasible, or even counterproductive. Change is difficult for most people, so doing things in a new way can feel threatening. Success becomes possible through change, so don't let the status quo defeat good ideas and new ways of doing things.

Find Good, Caring People to Collaborate With

Individuals with ASDs experience more than their fair share of rejection. Do not let unreturned greetings, unreciprocated invitations, or other social snubs deter you from looking for the community of caring people who will "get it" and join in your efforts. This applies to people in the community, school staff, and members of the peer group. They may be hard to find, but they are out there.

Make the Plan Fit the Individual, Not the Individual Fit the Plan

Sometimes our best efforts and ideas fail to bring success. We often look at the individual and think, "If only he would ..." or "Why doesn't he ...?" At these times it is important to go back to basics and look at the child's profile of strengths and ways of interacting with the world. Autism spectrum disorders present with a great deal of individual variation – each person is unique. We need to use these moments of frustration to figure out what we missed and what was left out of our plan instead of agonizing over what is wrong with the individual.

Realize That the Impact of Your Efforts Will Be Far Reaching

There has been a great deal of progress over the last 20 years in our efforts to help individuals with ASDs through designing new ways to facilitate development, providing effective instruction, managing difficult behaviors, and establishing integration into schools and communities. One essential ingredient of this progress has been the work of families and school teams in learning new skills, trying new strategies, and providing new types of support.

When you're working with individuals with ASDs, and especially when you're trying to intervene within the social environment, you are usually breaking new ground in these efforts toward progress. Even if gains for the individual are slow in coming, your work will make it easier for the next student who comes along. Programs you put in place will help the schools and families to become more effective in the long run and change the way everyone involved feels about ASDs. It is only through the efforts of people like you that we have been able to make the significant progress of the last 20 years and will continue to be successful at overcoming the challenges of autism spectrum disorders.

References

Baker, J. (2003). *Social skills training for children and adolescents with Asperger Syndrome and social-communication problems.* Shawnee Mission, KS: Autism Asperger Publishing Company.

Bellini, S. (2006). *Building social relationships: A systematic approach to teaching social interaction skills to children and adolescents with autism spectrum disorders and other social difficulties.* Shawnee Mission, KS: Autism Asperger Publishing Company.

Bellini, S. (in press). *Autism Social Skills Profile.* Shawnee Mission, KS: Autism Asperger Publishing Company.

Buron, K. D., & Curtis, M. (2003). *The incredible 5-point scale: Assisting students with autism spectrum disorders in understanding social interactions and controlling their emotional responses.* Shawnee Mission, KS: Autism Asperger Publishing Company.

Carter, A. S., Davis, N. O., Klin, A., & Volkmar, F. R. (2005). Social development in autism. In F. R. Volkmar, R. Paul, A. Klin, & D. Cohen (Eds.), *Handbook of autism and pervasive developmental disorders* (3rd ed., pp. 312-334). Hoboken, NJ: John Wiley and Sons.

Cooper, J. O., Heron, T. E., & Heward, W. L. (2007). *Applied behavior analysis* (2nd ed.). Upper Saddle River, NJ: Pearson.

Coucouvanis, J. (2004). *Super skills. A social skills group program for children with Asperger Syndrome, high-functioning autism and related challenges.* Shawnee Mission, KS: Autism Asperger Publishing Company.

Cowan, R. J., & Allen, K. D. (2007). Using naturalistic learning in individuals with autism: A focus on generalized teaching within the school setting. *Psychology in the Schools, 44*(7), 701-715.

Dunn, M. (2006). *S.O.S. – Social skills in our schools: A social skill program for children with pervasive developmental disorders and their typical peers.* Shawnee Mission, KS: Autism Asperger Publishing Company.

Freeman, S., & Dake, L. (1997). *Teach me language: A language manual for children with autism, Asperger's syndrome, and related developmental disorders.* Langley, British Columbia: SKF Books.

Gagnon, E. (2001). *Power Cards: Using special interests to motivate children and youth with Asperger Syndrome and autism.* Shawnee Mission, KS: Autism Asperger Publishing Company.

Gray, C. (1994). *Comic strip conversations: Colorful, illustrated interactions with students with autism and related disorders.* Jenison, MI: Jenison Public Schools.

Gray, C., & White, A. L. (2002). *My social stories book.* London: Jessica Kingsley Publishers.

Gresham, F. M. (2002). Social skills assessment and instruction for students with emotional and behavioral disorders. In K. L. Lane, F. M. Gresham, & T. E. O'Shaughnessy (Eds.), *Interventions for children with or at risk for emotional and behavioral disorders* (pp. 242-258). Boston: Allyn and Bacon.

Gresham, F. M., & Elliott, S. N. (1990). *Social Skills Rating System manual.* Circle Pines, MN: American Guidance Service.

Hodgdon, L. A. (1995). *Visual strategies for improving communication: Practical supports for school and home.* Troy, MI: Quirk Roberts Publishing.

Hudson, J., & Coffin, B. C. (2007). *Out and about: Preparing children with autism spectrum disorders to participate in their communities.* Shawnee Mission, KS: Autism Asperger Publishing Company.

McAfee, J. (2002). *Navigating the social world: A curriculum for individuals with Asperger's Syndrome, high functioning autism, and related disorders.* Arlington, TX: Future Horizons.

Merrell, K. W. (2002). *School Social Behavior Scales: User's guide* (2nd ed.). Eugene, OR: Assessment-Intervention Resources.

Myles, B. S., & Southwick, J. (2005). *Asperger syndrome and difficult moments: Practical solutions for tantrums, rage and meltdowns.* Shawnee Mission, KS: Autism Asperger Publishing Company.

Myles, B. S., Trautman, M. L., & Schelvan, R. L. (2004). *The hidden curriculum: Practical solutions for understanding unstated rules in social situations.* Shawnee Mission, KS: Autism Asperger Publishing Company.

PL 93-112 (1973) The Rehabilitation Act of 1973, Sec. 504.

PL 108-46 (2004) Individuals with Disabilities Education Improvement Act (IDEA).

Quill, K. A. (2000). *Do-watch-listen-say: Social and communication intervention for children with autism.* Baltimore: Paul H. Brookes Publishing.

Rogers, S. J., Cook, I., & Meryl, A. (2005). Imitation and play in autism. In F. R. Volkmar, R. Paul, A. Klin, & D. Cohen (Eds.), *Handbook of autism and pervasive developmental disorders* (3rd ed., pp. 382-405*).* Hoboken, NJ: John Wiley and Sons.

Schlieder, M. S. (2007). *With open arms: Creating school communities of support for kids with social challenges using Circle of Friends, extracurricular activities, and learning teams.* Shawnee Mission, KS: Autism Asperger Publishing Company.

Schopler, E., & Mesibov, G. B. (Eds.). (1986). *Social behavior in autism.* New York: Plenum Press.

Schreibman, L., & Ingersoll, B. (2005). Behavioral interventions to promote learning in individuals with autism. In F. Volkmar, R. Paul, A. Klin, & D. Cohen (Eds.), *Handbook of autism and pervasive developmental disorders, Vol. 2: Assessment, interventions and policy* (3rd ed., pp. 882-896). Hoboken, NJ: John Wiley and Sons.

Stone, W. L., & LaGreca, A. M. (1986). The development of social skills in children. In E. Schopler & G. Mesibov (Eds.), *Social behavior in autism* (pp. 35-60). New York: Plenum Press.

Timler, G. R., Vogler-Elias, D., & McGill, K. F. (2007). Strategies for promoting generalization of social communication skills in pre-schoolers and school-aged children. *Topics in Language Disorders, 27*(2), 167-181.

Wagner, S. (1999). *Inclusive programming for elementary students with autism.* Arlington, TX: Future Horizons.

Winner, M. G. (2002). *Thinking about you, thinking about me: Philosophy and strategies to further develop perspective taking and communicative abilities for persons with social cognitive deficits.* San Jose, CA: Author.

Index

APC

Autism Asperger Publishing Company
P.O. Box 23173
Shawnee Mission, Kansas 66283-0173
www.asperger.net